A PERFECT SEASON

by

Daniel L Kobylinski

Copyright 2021 Daniel L Kobylinski
ISBN 978-1-7377013-0-9

All rights reserved. No part of this book shall be reproduced or used in any manner without the prior written permission of the author, except for the use of brief quotations in a book review.

For all the really good coaches out there who give their time and skill to respectfully teach their players a sport and positively teach them about life.

FORWARD

I wrote this book to tell the story about a Perfect Season in 1981. It is a story about a small-town group of farm kids in Central Minnesota who believed their football coach when he told them they could be champions, and that Legendary Coach who brought order, discipline, professionalism, and victory to the team. It is also about life in the 80s in small town Minnesota.

I wasn't a writer when I began this project. I didn't want to wait until I became a writer to write it, because that may never happen. So, I just sat down and put the story to words in the best way I could. I apologize in advance for inconsistencies in flow and pace. Those are writing terms and since I'm not (yet) a writer, it may or may not have good flow and pace.

This book describes events that occurred around 40 years ago. It seems that memories aren't perfect after 40 years. The events like scores and statistics are based on facts. Some of the stories are based on memory. When possible, I attempted to verify accounts with more than one person. So, if I got anything wrong, I do apologize. But these accounts are accurate to the best of our collective memories.

Prologue

On Friday, November 13th, 1981 the undefeated Holdingford Huskers were in a battle to save their season. Would this Friday the 13th be a nightmare or a celebration?

The high school football team was losing 14-7, and the opposing team had the ball in our territory, with only eight minutes left in the game. Things didn't look good for the mighty Huskers.

We found ourselves in an unusual position since we hadn't lost a game all year. We had never even trailed once in the 10 games we had played. We had only given up two touchdowns in those ten games. And this undefeated Mahnomen team already had two against us, plus they were methodically moving the ball and close to scoring a third one. Most of the people from Holdingford were on the sidelines for the game in Mahnomen, Minnesota.

I was a tenth grader on the team observing from the sideline. Along with hundreds of other Husker's fans we were painfully watching as our season was slowly slipping away. Things didn't look good! But the stars aligned for us or fate smiled upon us that night and we won the Mahnomen game 21-14.

This is the story about the 1981 team and the legendary Holdingford football coach who led us through an undefeated season to Holdingford's first and only state championship up to that point.

Chapter 1- Practice

The season began in mid-August. We started practice in the mornings before school was in session. It was an exciting time for a kid like me; my first year to dress for the varsity team. I had no illusions about starting or even playing on varsity. I hadn't seen a lot of my friends all summer and getting together was always fun. A lot of us worked on farms over the summer so we were in pretty good shape, a good thing since Coach Roebuck was known for his conditioning drills. That was a big part of our practices. His 4th quarter drills were not enjoyable, yet paid dividends about three months later.

Since the first game of the season was usually on the first Friday after school started, which was usually after Labor Day, we began practices a couple weeks prior. There were around fifty-five players out for the team from grades ten, eleven, and twelve.

Most players drove cars and carpooled to the morning practices. All the cars were parked by the back door of the school, closest to the locker room. Some of the players from St. Wendell and other surrounding areas carpooled with six or seven people in the car.

August in Minnesota is a hot month. We practiced early in the morning, to avoid the steaming hot midday heat. The grass often had dew on it in the morning, but as the sun rose the temperature warmed up quickly. That first day we were issued our gear. We tried on helmets and made sure they fit, and we received our shoulder pads and practice pants. We were assigned lockers and would be responsible for our equipment until the season ended.

Head coach, Gary Roebuck, planned practices to the minute, and we could see the schedule every day before practice started. Coach Roebuck was a consummate professional, down to the last detail. Even though this was high school he coached like he was in the NFL. His professionalism trickled down to us and every player practiced with the proper type of intensity... eventually.

The early days were designed to set the tone for the season. Which meant no screwing around. No half-assing drills. Often during these early season practices some players would not take drills seriously. That never went over well with a serious coach like Roebuck. As a player, you learned quickly if you wanted to play, you took practice and drills seriously. The day-to-day details may be a little vague but practice had a normal rhythm. It started with stretching. Then a little running to warm up. Then practice drills per your position. Then practice plays. Then 4thquarter drills and other conditioning sessions. Then more practice plays, while you are tired.

One of the drills we did was 4 stations at the four corners of the field. Everyone was separated in to four groups and started at one of the corners. At one corner you would do burpees or something like that. Then at the whistle you would run full speed to the next corner where you might do pushups and sit-ups. Then at the whistle run full speed to the next corner and do another drill, and so on until the coaches were ready for a break.

Mostly the juniors and seniors worked with varsity and us sophomores practiced on the JV team. Gary Roebuck was the head coach and his assistants were Roman Pierskalla and Dale Bruns. So, we ran our plays and learned our positions. I played wide receiver on JV. Sounds good but passing was not a big part of high school football around this time. I also got some playing time as a cornerback.

My participation in the 1981 season was the result of growing up in a football-playing and Minnesota Vikings-watching family. I didn't realize it at the time, but not all families watched football on Sundays or played football with the neighbors in the fall. But our family did. Our family watched the Vikings on Sundays on an old black and white TV. Back then we were fans of Fran Tarkenton, Chuck Foreman, Sammy White, and Ahmad Rashad. With Jeff Siemen, Paul Krause, and the Purple People Eaters on defense. The Vikings went to the Super Bowl 4 times during this period. They didn't win any but who's keeping track? (Everyone in Wisconsin.)

Holdingford is about 100 miles northwest of Minneapolis and St. Paul. Pure farm country. Coach Roebuck didn't seem like a small-town coach. He seemed more like a big city guy. He was a natural leader and most every player respected him and his football philosophy without question. He was from North Dakota and he carried himself with a sort of assumed confidence and as we were mostly small-town farm kids and were still taught to respect adults, coach Roebuck was a natural authority figure to us all. Authority figure and one most everyone respected and admired.

As a sixteen-year-old growing up in a football-watching family, playing on the varsity team was an exciting time.

My journey to this team started on a small farm two miles outside of Holdingford. On the farm we milked cows, and had pigs and chickens and usually one or two loyal farm dogs. Farm work never ended. All the animals needed to be fed every day. The cows were milked twice a day, every day. All the pens had to be cleaned. In the spring, fields needed to be prepared and crops needed to be planted. All summer crops were tended too and hay was bailed. The hay was bailed and then stacked in the hay barn.

In the fall the crops were harvested, and wood was cut and loaded and stacked in the basement and around the house for the cold winter. Our house was heated with wood; a big wood furnace in the basement. No electric heat. So, there always had to be enough wood cut. On a farm there is always work to do, and we were kept busy. As a result, we were in good shape.

My mom also planted a huge garden in the spring. Her vegetables, with a focus on potatoes—and I mean a lot of potatoes—were harvested in the fall, and then canned and frozen for food all winter. My recollection is that we had potatoes for at least two meals a day, and sometimes three, for the first eighteen years of my life (a slight exaggeration but we had potatoes a lot). Boiled, baked, fried, French fried, au gratin, mashed, pancakes—which were everyone's favorite— but mostly boiled and served with gravy. And it is also my contention that after I left home at eighteen, I didn't eat potatoes for about twenty years. I did have the occasional French fries with my burgers, and I sometimes ate potato pancakes with cottage cheese. They were always great, and still are, but for the most part I didn't have a taste for potatoes.

From a young age, I remember playing football with my older brothers in our yard or neighbors' yards on Sundays in the fall. We had a fairly big yard, and our neighbors to the South, the Wentland's had a great yard for football. It was large and rectangular. With a row of bushes on one side representing the sideline, and a driveway on the other side as the other sideline. There was a ditch for one end zone, and on the other end we threw two articles of clothing to represent the other end zone.

Sometimes Myron Feia or Jim and Larry Hadley played with us and occasionally a Bieniek or a Pilarski. Sometimes other neighbors or relatives joined our pick-up games. The players varied from week to week. I recall myself and Gary Wentland—who I have known since kindergarten—were always in attendance. We tried to get an even number of players, (i.e., six or eight), but that didn't always work, so we occasionally had lopsided teams of three against four. We simply made up some rules to make it fair. Maybe there would be a kid who always played quarterback. Or maybe the team with more players, couldn't rush. Then we timed the play and the quarterback had to pass within five seconds or so. We would do whatever to keep the game going. A game could last a couple hours. We would drink water from the hose in the yard. We would be wearing old worn, hand-me-down clothes and since we played tackle football, sometimes our shirts would be torn and shredded. After the games, we would bike home and eat meat, potatoes, and other vegetables.

When I was thirteen, my parents retired from farming, and we moved two miles into the town of Holdingford. My brother Bob and his wife Alice took over the farm and I was free labor for the next 6 years.   So, when I started 7th grade, we were living in Holdingford. We could start playing organized tackle football. Roman Pierskalla was the coach of the 7th grade team. In 7th and 8th grade it seems we only played 5 or 6 games. It was mostly about having fun and learning about football. In the 8th grade, our Coach was Dick Carlson, who was the English teacher and drama club director. He had a unique philosophy. Since it was about having fun and since we had around 20 players out for the team, everyone played. You played either offense or defense. With a couple players playing both sides, on a rotating basis.

For me, perhaps the most enjoyable year for playing football was the 9th grade. Greg White was the coach. I remember I played every play of every game. Offense, defense, and special teams. Every single play. Never during the year was I on the sideline once the game started. I seem to remember only playing five games and being 3-2, but for me it was fun because I just liked playing and never got tired.

On the 1981 team there were around fifty-five kids out for football, which means only eleven to twenty-two players would be first team starters. That left a lot of players on the sidelines. On our team that year, there were seven or eight seniors who started both on offense and defense, leaving even less. Coach Roebuck was known for getting as many players into the game as possible. There are several reasons why this is smart. First, the more players who are out for the team, the more talent the coach has to choose from. Second, having more kids out for the team is also building experience for the future. And third, it gives the coach more players to run better scrimmages during practice. Wise coaches know this. If kids aren't getting any playing time or aren't having fun, they won't come out for sports.

There is a fine line between fielding your best team and trying to get more players into the game. In our year of greatness, a lot of players saw playing time, especially all the seniors. As a sophomore we didn't have illusions of playing a lot in varsity games. Although, we did get into most games in the 4th quarter because we routed so many teams.

*

Addendum

I want to close out each chapter with a story as it relates to life in the 1980s in small town central Minnesota. These are simply goofy stories that set the tone for the era. This was four decades ago.

As we were living in the 80s as teenagers, we did things that we thought were normal. You kind of go through your teenage years feeling your way to the next step. It is all new and we were just learning as we went. We did what our friends were doing. We did what seemed like fun. We went to parties. We had some beers. As the saying goes, teenagers think they are invincible and sometimes do really dumb things. I certainly have done some dumb things. At the time they didn't seem too bad. Though now, 40 years later, as I look back at some of the things we did, I can see were pretty dumb. But they also make for funny stories. So, at the end of each chapter, I will finish the chapter with what I consider a funny story about the life and times of a teenager in central Minnesota during the 1980s based on my experiences.

It will be called "Story Alert-Life in the 80s." Some are funny, and some are crazy, and some are neither, but all are true.

STORY ALERT - LIFE IN THE 80s

Keeping in line with people exaggerating their childhood, I will add my two cents. Everyone makes claims about how tough they had it growing up. You know, walking to school in the snow, uphill both ways. We grew up in the country and in fact all my older siblings did have to walk to the one room school house a little less than one mile down the road. This was before the big high school was built in Holdingford. They had to walk to school at least for a couple years. I was the first one to actually start kindergarten in the elementary school in town. I never had to walk to the one room schoolhouse, though I did follow my siblings there once as a three- or four-year-old. So, I had to come up with some other stories to impress the next generation with how hard we had it. Picking rocks at four. Baling hay at five. Driving a tractor at seven. Driving a farm truck at nine.

One of the stories I still tell often is about having to carry cows and calves across the creek. This one is, in fact, based on some actual events and I may as well use this opportunity to set the record straight.

In the spring cows usually have their babies. Most farms have a big wood for cows to wander around and find grass to eat. There are trees and hills and you can't always see the cows. Around supper time the cows usually make their way back to the barn because they know they will be fed, and milked.

One day one of our cows was missing. She was due to have a baby and my brother sent me out to find it and bring them back. I was probably thirteen or fourteen. I found the cow way in the back forty, as we say. And, she did have a little baby with her. Likely born within the last few hours. The babies can usually walk and nurse within an hour of birth but are not very coordinated. The mom usually licks them to clean them up as she waits for it to stand up. The babies can walk but would prefer to lay down, unless being fed, because they were just born and don't have a lot of energy. We were a long way from the barn. Our loyal farm dog Fuzzy was there to monitor things. Incidentally, Fuzzy was a very smart farm dog. Purebred mutt and very protective of us humans. The plan was to start walking the cow toward the barn and the calf would follow. The cows were quite docile and generally not aggressive. As we started towards the farm, it was a slow process. The cow kept looking back for the calf. The calf clumsily tried to keep up. He kept lying down for a break. Then we came to the first creek. It was a small, shallow creek but there was water flowing. It seemed the quickest way to cross was to pick up the calf to my front and carry him across. The cow looked at me but understands we are all friends here. That worked. We still had a long way to go and one more small creek to cross. The calf stumbled along as we went but it was taking too long.

I had to make a decision. I would say we were 600-700 yards from the farm. I decided I needed to carry the calf. So, making sure mom cow was cool with it, I picked up the calf and put it over my shoulders with his legs hanging down my chest. The calf didn't seem to mind as he just relaxed and we headed for home. Newborn calves are 60-80 lbs or so. Mom followed along closely and bellowed a few times. Like I said we crossed one more creek, and were back at the barn. I set the calf down and mom inspected him to make sure all was ok. Mom and calf both relaxed and both were able to get some well-deserved supper. This has nothing to do with football, but I did in fact carry a baby cow across the creek. All true, though in the embellished version the creek was a raging river and the calf weighed twice as much.

Chapter 2 – Players

There were a lot of farm boys on our team. Every kid was either from a farm, lived in the country, or lived in a town with fewer than 600 people. Holdingford, a town of 621 people, had the High School. Kids from within 15 miles or so came to this school. There were a couple other small towns within a few miles of Holdingford, but Holdingford was their school district. Towns like St. Anna, St. Wendell, Opole, and Arban all fed kids to the Holdingford school district. Arban is an interesting town. Not so much a town, as an idea. If you get a chance to take a day trip to Arban, I am sure you will "find" the town welcoming.

The Ertl boys. Jim and Bill. Visualize two big, strong Norwegian farm kids. Except they were German. So may as well visualize 2 big strong German farm kids. Minnesota is sort of known as having many people of Swedish and Norwegian descent. Which is true in large areas of the state. Remember Sven and Ole and Lena jokes? However, there are big groups of people with German and Polish descent. Our little area around

Holdingford is fairly evenly divided between German and Polish ancestry.

As for Polish on the team we had Harvey Wenderski, Steve Malikowski, Randy Piechowski, Scott Yurczyk, Chad Woidylla, Leon and Mike Opatz, Ron, Sam and Irv Pierskalla and others.

Back to Jim and Bill. All these kids wanted to do was play football. Even in high school, they both seemed set to stay on at the farm. No college plans. No military or job plans. Farming was in their DNA. They would likely end up on the family farm. Playing football in high school would be a big part of their life. And they were dedicated. These were the kind of kids that did exactly what the coach asked of them.

Being respectful of their elders, they had no intention of letting down the coach or their family. Kids like this are the dream of any smart coach. A smart coach wants strong kids who are smart and are teachable and do as they are told. There is never any back-talk from kids like this. Never. But there are other kids who may be a bit less inclined toward authority. All teams likely have all varieties and personalities of players.

So, on any team there can be some resentment towards authority. Some kids are rebellious. Some like sports but are anti-authority. On this team in 1981, I remember not too much of that. There likely was some resentment but for the most part it never showed up.

I grew up on a farm like the Ertl boys. But if they were destined to be farmers, I was the absolute opposite of that. I had no interest in farming, I was a dreamer and bit of a reader. We had an old set of encyclopedias. In the P's was a picture of the leaning tower of Pisa. And I immediately wanted to see it. (And I did so in 1991.) Perhaps that is the beginning of my desire to travel. Life on the farm was busy and consistent. Busy is not conducive to dreaming. And dreaming is not conducive with safety on a farm. I was a dreamer and couldn't wait to see the world. Over the years there had been a few accidents and injuries on the farm. But we all left the farm with all our digits, though a few scars here and there.

On the sideline there were a wide range of players with differing abilities. Some big, some strong, some fast, and some were strong and fast. But there was also the other side of the spectrum. Kids go out for sports for a variety of reasons. And the team needs as many players as possible. As long as you give your best and complete the conditioning drills, you will be an accepted part of the team. This is the beauty of high school sports. Anyone in the 10th-12th grade who wanted to be on the team was on the team. Of course, all the jocks were on the team, but so were some other players, who may not have possessed great talent.

Junior, Terry Posch, was a good example of this. Terry Posch was the Rudy Ruettiger of the team. He was all heart. He was slow and not much for football ability, but he showed up every day. He gave his all during the scrimmages and conditioning drills. I like to think we were a pretty welcoming team. Ability was not the deciding factor on being accepted. Being a complainer or not putting in effort were the deciding factors. Doing all the drills and trying your hardest was the only requirement. The first several weeks of practice are physically intense. Lots of fitness drills to get everyone in shape. Terry showed up every day, like all of us. He played on defense against the 1st team offense. He got knocked down but he always got back up. He ran the drills. He was often last. But he finished. He was a good example of showing up every day without illusions of starting, he just wanted to be on the team, and he was. He did everything asked of him. And he never quit and never complained. Everyone fully accepted him as a part of the team.

Scott Radtke went to Army basic training in the summer before his senior year. He came back with an Army crew cut and some entertaining army songs. They were something like: I wish all the ladies, were bells in a tower, and I was a bellboy…. You can guess the last phrase. It seems to me these melodies caused some consternation in the office of the school. They were certainly frowned upon and may have been banned.

Mark Nentl, the team's big tackle, worked on a gold mine in Alaska the summer before his senior year. He worked for a friend of his dad's. They worked 7 days a week all summer.

Sophomore Tim Brown was listed at 120 lbs. By the time he was a senior he had gained 40-50 lbs.

Junior Ken Fedor was a 130 lbs farm kid. He just liked being on the team. He knew then his goal was to be a trucker and to own his truck. On the bus rides to games, he claims he sat up front to watch the bus driver and learn how to shift while listening to the engine.

There were some people who may be considered heavyset. In football they often make useful linemen. So, football teams have players of all sizes. Big guys don't usually win many of the running drills, which is fine. They just need to finish them. Their size is an asset on the line, whether offense or defense. We had big guys and we had scrappy 130 pounders as well.

And then of course were the three-sport athletes that make up the starters of any team. We will get to them shortly.

Also on this team were seven sets of brothers. Brian and Steve Danzl. Jim and Bill Ertl. Leon and Mike Opatz. Ron and Dan Fiedler. Todd and Tim Brown. Brian and Allan Reis. Ron and Sam Pierskalla, and their cousin Irv Pierskalla.

Our school was fairly small so everyone pretty much knew everyone else.

STORY ALERT - LIFE IN THE 80s

During one of the early 80s football seasons some players started a tradition that lasted for 3 weeks. There was a restaurant Called Noah's Ark a few miles west of Holdingford, and they had an all you could eat chicken special one night a week. So, after practice, when us growing kids were super hungry, a group of us went to check it out. We had 2 car loads of kids. There were maybe six or eight of us high school kids and they gave us a big table. We ordered the special which included a soda pop. Now if you can picture our group of practically starving kids after football practice and some of us were big linemen, we were hungry and ate a lot. The chicken was really good and we kept ordering. I remember the chicken bones piling up on the center of the table. I mean high stacks of bones. Finally, when we were all full, we headed home. For us this was a great deal and a cheap meal. We did this three weeks in a row. However, the owners didn't appreciate our appetite, and after the 3rd week, told us not to come back. That's only part of this story.

On the way home after one of these meals, we acted too much like teenage kids. There were two cars and I was in the second one. I believe Gene Ostendorf was driving and maybe Chad Woidylla and others were in our car. I believe it was Bill Shank and Jeff Stoermann and others in the first car. Well, as we were heading back to Holdingford, we were probably flipping birds at each other and one thing led to another. Keep in mind they were likely driving at least 55 mph. (As we all know, teenage kids with their friends drive the speed limit.) Let us naively assume we were driving 55 mph. These are small quiet country roads. No other towns around. Just farms every few miles and with farm fields on either side of the road. There are some curves and some small hills. But pretty quiet roads without much other traffic.

Slowly and deliberately, Jeff Stoermann comes out of the passenger side window of the first car. Our curiosity peaked as we were wondering what was going to happen. First, he was sitting on the window with his legs still inside the car. Wind was blowing his hair as he contemplated his next move. I thought that should be enough.

Nope.

He kept going sort of clinging close to the car as he made his way up into the top of the car. One hand on the front, and one hand on the top of the window he just came out of. He was sort of half in and half out. I thought that was definitely enough.

Nope.

With one hand, carefully he undoes his pants and slides the back of his pants down just enough to moon us. Not a full moon, like if you were standing on solid ground not moving. But enough to be considered a moon. On the top of the car, at 55 mph! I thought he displayed extreme coordination and dexterity.

He wasn't out there very long, but long enough to set the standard of extreme foolishness, that I believe shouldn't be and hope won't be topped. And then he slowly and carefully made his way back in. This is a true story and also a case study verifying that sixteen- and seventeen-year-old brains aren't fully developed yet... Although we thought it was pretty funny at the time.

Chapter 3 - Pre-Season

When I started researching for this book, I wanted to speak with as many players as I could. One of the questions I asked people was: Were there high expectations for this team before the season began? The answer was yes. The seniors on the 1981 team had only lost five games in total since the 7th grade. They lost once in the 9th grade to Albany which was a much bigger school, and twice each in the 10th and 11th grades. The year before when they were juniors they lost one game during the season, and one game in the playoffs to Mahnomen who went on to win the state championship. As a grade they were bringing back 7 starters on defense and 5 starters on offense. I didn't realize this as a sophomore. But this team knew they would be good, and really wanted to make a run for the title.

There were about eight teams in a conference. In 1981, only one team per conference made the playoffs. Holdingford had won the conference 3 of the last 4 years. 1977, 1979, 1980. The last two years losing to Mahnomen in the semifinals. The expectation was to certainly win the conference and go to the playoffs.

Imagine the coach instilling in the minds of his players, over several years, that winning was the expectation. To me that seems like a positive thing to plant in a young person's mind. But Coach Roebuck did it the right way. No cutting corners, no cheating. You achieved victory by being prepared, by practicing correctly, and by conditioning. He would adjust his offense and defense schemes to the players on hand. When you have a big line, you can power up the middle. When you have a smaller and quicker line you go more to the outside to get into the open field.

After talking to some of the players, it turns out the captains and the leaders of the team sat down with the other seniors and explained this was going to be a special year. That the players needed to follow all the team rules throughout the season and not jeopardize a suspension by doing anything stupid. In those days, the something stupid was drinking alcohol or maybe fighting in school.

Based on my own experience, occasional parties happened throughout the year. Also, there were bars and clubs around. When I say clubs, I don't mean clubs like what comes to mind today... I mean a building with a door, a bar, and a stage for bands. Nothing fancy, but in the 80s it was a place to go see a band in our country area that allowed students in. The other local joke was that every town in the area had one church and at least one bar.

Generally, you weren't served alcohol at these places, unless of course, you had a fake ID or looked old enough. And since the bar owners were there to make money, and underage drinking enforcement wasn't a high priority, they didn't really care how old you looked. But even then, we usually brought our own beer or had some beers before going to the place. I remember Dino's in Avon, the New Munich ballroom and another ballroom in St. Anna, which is still there today.

So, parties and alcohol were pretty common. I honestly can say during my grades 7-12 I never saw or was exposed to marijuana or any other drugs. There was booze but never any drugs. This was small town farm country in Minnesota in the 80s. Kegs yes, drugs that I witnessed, none. That's not to say there weren't any, I just never saw any.

The team leaders knew this was going to be a special season. The senior captains were Dale Mehr, Brian Reis and Ron Fiedler. Other leaders on the team were Dan Stich, Mark Nentl, Dan Sobieck, and Brian Danzl. They encouraged all the seniors to not drink and follow all the team rules for about the 4 months of the fall season. That really shows leadership for these seventeen and eighteen-year-old kids. The team leaders understood that all the linemen and other position players were an integral part of the team, and losing the wrong person for a few games could be bad for the team.

I loved playing football. I wouldn't do anything stupid to risk getting caught. Having some beers even at family functions was pretty normal back then, at least in my family. But it turns out most players simply followed the rules through the season. I said most. After interviewing a lot of people, it turns out not everyone followed all the rules.

After speaking with Dale Mehr, he plainly explained that winning in Holdingford had become a tradition. It was an expectation. That came from Coach Roebucks singular focus since he arrived in Holdingford, to build a football program. To build a winning tradition. He recruited players. He aligned with the booster club. He even spent a lot of time preparing the football field. There are stories of the coach going out to farms and speaking with the parents of kids he wanted to recruit. Sometimes they joined the team and sometimes they didn't. He spent a lot of time building the football program in Holdingford.

Most of the players' journey to the 1981 season began within fifteen miles of Holdingford. Gary and Jane Roebuck's journey to central Minnesota started several hundred miles away in a little town in North Dakota.

Gary Roebuck grew up in a small town called Velva North Dakota. According to his wife Jane, Gary was an outstanding athlete in high school and college. He played other sports besides football. He was a couple years older than Jane, and she was friends with Gary's sister. They knew each other in high school but didn't start dating until he was a sophomore at Minot State University. When she graduated high school, she also went to Minot State University. When Gary graduated college, he ended up teaching and coaching in a little town called Fessenden North Dakota. In 1963, Gary and Jane were married.

As he was a pretty young football coach and Fessenden was in the same conference as Velva, Coach Roebuck ended up coaching against his younger brother who was the quarterback at Velva High School.

Gary and Jane were at Fessenden for 6 years. As the story goes, S.L. Tuchscherer was a coach in North Dakota and was in the same circle of coaches as Coach Roebuck. Eventually, Tuchscherer ended up in Holdingford, Minnesota. Around 1969 Tuchscherer recruited Gary to come to Holdingford to be a teacher and coach. And that is where the Roebucks remained for 15 years.

When Coach Roebuck became the football coach in Holdingford, the team had gone 2-3 years with very few wins. Dale Bruns stated Coach Roebuck developed a football program when he came to Holdingford. When he arrived in 1969 the team was not very good. Coach Roebuck focused on getting more kids out for football. Also starting them earlier so they had some experience when they became seniors.

He was a long-term thinker and started this process when he arrived in 1969 which quickly bore fruit in 1973. Within four years of Coach Roebuck arriving in Holdingford, the Huskers played for a state championship, losing to Gaylord, MN. It took another eight years for the team to make it to a championship game. But the point is, in his years there as a Coach, he developed a program and developed players which led to years of winning seasons for Holdingford. Which is unlike some schools, of similar enrollment, without a dedicated coach and they suffered years of losing seasons.

Keep in mind Coach Roebuck had a full-time job at the school, and coaching was a part time gig after school. He was one of those coaches who lived and breathed coaching football. His dedication to the sport and the players of Holdingford left an indelible mark in the lives of those who were fortunate enough to play for him.

The system in Minnesota is similar to other states as it relates to which class a team will be in. It is based on student enrollment in the school.

The Minnesota State High School League Determines the class structure. In 1981 there were five classes based on enrollment. There were AA, A, B, C, and 9 man. Holdingford was in Class B.

Per Wikipedia: "Because of the large number of high schools and large distances spanned between some of them, many schools are organized into conferences. These conferences, which, according to Minnesota State High School League rules, must have a minimum of five members, are usually composed of schools that are in close geographic proximity and have similar enrollments. During the regular season, a school plays a number of its games against other teams in its conference (this number varies depending on the sport and conference in question)."

Keep in mind, Holdingford was playing schools with a similar enrollment. The student class size for our school was about 100 kids per grade. That was the average. That was likely very similar to the other schools in all of class B. The difference was the team's coach.

Holdingford didn't realize how lucky they were to land Coach Roebuck. Wherever he ended up would be a town that would see their football program turned into a powerhouse. Fortunately, he took the job before he even visited Holdingford. That was in 1969.

He crafted the concept that football on Friday nights was a town event. He got the community involved. It was Coach Roebuck who made the games an event, and made it cool to play football. During the summer, when school was out, he spent a lot of his extra time working on the field. He was the one who painted the lines on the field, along with the help of his kids, Jeff and Renee. He was meticulous with the uniforms and the helmets. Each year he and his kids painted the helmets and attached the Holdingford H. He raised standards with the practices and the games.

Some coaches use conditioning as a punishment. If someone screws up or if the team isn't performing well, they punish the team by running them. The problem in my mind is that if they only treat conditioning as a punishment, then the team starts to resent doing it because a coach then needs an excuse to make the players run. However, running and conditioning are a crucial part to sport preparation. When you make it part of practice, and you emphasize the benefits of it, the team will understand the why, and hopefully do it with a better attitude. Because as I may have mentioned, running really hard for longer than is comfortable and doing three person drop and flop (Husker Rolls) aren't fun while doing them.

The Husker roll was designed for 3 people. At the start whistle the middle person drops and rolls one way. As he rolls toward the outside guy, that guy dives over him and rolls toward the 3rd person. The 3rd person dives and rolls toward the 1st guy, who needs to be up and ready and he dives over and rolls. And you keep going until the coach gets tired. The idea is for speed. As soon as you dive and roll, you need to pop up and immediately dive and roll the other way, and so on. Coach Roebuck put them on the schedule and we knew they were coming. They weren't punishment. They were a part of practice that made us better.

Another of those exercises was wind sprints or 4x40's. Basically all the backs and receivers lined up on one side of the practice field, and on go, would run 40-50 yards to the other side of the field, touch the line, come back to this side, touch the line, and once more back and forth. And it was timed. Then the offensive and defensive lineman would line up and do the same.

The linemen were usually bigger and slower. There were some quick linemen, such as Lee Odden who was pretty big and strong, and also fast. He got to run with the backs and receivers, which would be more of a challenge. On the line we had a few big-bodied kids. They usually brought up the rear. Speed was not their asset, pushing opposing players around was their purpose.

I remember one time, during another year, I believe it was Tim Kolstad, who was running with the lineman. Not a big kid so he was usually closer to the front of the pack. As he was coming back to touch the line on the near side of the field, he missed the line, and Coach Roebuck saw this. The Coach yelled and said to come back and re-touch the line. This all took a few seconds, so by now he was in the back of the pack. He still had to go down and back, so another 100 yards. The coach started yelling, you better not be last, and don't go over the time limit. Previously, since he was faster than the pack he could cruise along. Now since he was behind and couldn't be the last person, he had to pick up the pace. I'm guessing he was chasing Frank Sewart and Terry Posch. Neither were the fastest but both had heart. I don't know for sure but in my mind, I hope that they kicked it up a notch as well, to see if they could beat Tim. Speaking of heart, Tim Kolstad had that. Never the biggest kid but he had heart and he was as scrappy as anyone.

As the linemen are running everyone else stands on the line waiting for their turn to come up again.

Everyone could hear and see what was happening. Tim was way behind and he couldn't be last. The team started cheering, or maybe heckling, but definitely some form of yelling. Telling him to hurry and that he better not be last. The way I remember it was a photo finish as Tim was running full speed to the line and dove across it airborne. And he did it under the time limit. That to me was just a simple example of a player with heart laying it all out there to do the drill correctly. Incidentally, Tim Kolstad who was maybe 5'5" and 145 lbs, was tough and scrappy enough to become an all-conference guard as a senior.

It seems we always did some sort of conditioning at every practice, except maybe on Thursdays, the day before the game, when we practiced in shoulder pads and shorts. There was generally no hitting on Thursdays.

After practice in the summer a lot of kids showered and then went downtown to the local grocery store and bought some pop (soda) or snacks and hung out on main street for a while before heading home. Mainstreet Holdingford was two blocks long, with two grocery stores, two hardware stores, two or three bars and one cafe.

Once the school year started practices happened after school at about 3:45. The last class of the day was around 3:15. The conversations in the locker room before and after practice were always entertaining.

And I had a front row seat.

I lived in town and I drove my black 1965 Pontiac Catalina to school. After practice, when all the other kids were rushing to catch the late bus for a ride home, or some of the farm kids who had a car were rushing to get home for farm chores, I would take my time and hang around the locker room and catch up on all the gossip. Mostly it was players laughing and joking around.

All the seniors were involved in these antics. But Ron Fiedler and Dan Stich were the most boisterous. They were great friends then and are still to this day. They loved to argue. They always had big and contrary opinions and lots of comedy. As a sophomore, I didn't say much but usually just listened to the banter. The times in the locker room after practice are still some of the things I remember most about that year. It was always comical, often sarcastic, and sometimes insulting. Also being the very naive kid that I was, I didn't always understand what they were talking about. But I pretended I did so as not to appear to be such dork. I remember laughing a lot.

When it came to sex talk, which it did occasionally, I would listen in so as to learn something. Hey, that's where we learned things! I couldn't just ask someone what things meant because that would make me look like a complete naïve idiot, which I was but I didn't want others to know it.

People were ruthless in their sarcastic criticism. It would become a mob criticism usually all in fun and not in vitriolic meanness, but definitely in subtle meanness. And so, it wasn't fun being the brunt of the jokes when that occasionally happened. Usually, the sarcasm traveled from person to person and everyone got their share.

Kids can be ruthless. As kids this age were still criticizing for the benefit of making others look stupid in the vain attempt to bring themselves up. As adults we now understand what was happening. We understand teenage group dynamics, but as a teenager you never wanted to be singled out in ruthless jokes or heavy criticism. But you also didn't want to miss out on the gossip or the comedy.

There were a lot of Dan's on the team. Over 33% of the Seniors were named Dan; six of the seventeen. Just Seniors. There was Dan Stich, Dan Koehn, Dan Bieniek, Dan Gill, Dan Dickhausen, and Dan Sobieck. And two more of us sophomores, Dan Fiedler and myself. I remember once in the locker room, as the banter went anywhere and everywhere, this anomaly came up when some were talking about all the Dan's. Ron Fiedler, in his role as ambassador of smart ass and employing a bit of wordplay said: "A lot of Dan's and none worth a damn."

One little initiation for rookies (10th graders) on the varsity team were the occasional hazing rituals. Right after school all the players went to the locker room, changed and headed out to the practice field.

We took the same route every day. From the locker room there was a hallway to a back door of the school. All the players would walk this hallway in their socks carrying their shoes so as not to get the hallway floor dirty. Then just outside the door we put our cleats on. Then out onto the grass. The actual game field was off to the right about 100 yards away. But the practice field was off to the left 200-300 yards away. It was an old grass field with cornfields on two sides. Everyone casually walked out there at their own pace in a long line of individuals and small groups.

There were usually five to ten minutes before the coaches showed up, so this is when things happened. The older classmen would line up in two rows as we entered the practice field. Everyone as they showed up had to go between the two rows and they shoved and pushed and tried to knock us down. If you were a smart ass the shoving got more intense. Gary Wentland, my old neighbor, who was a stocky and strong farm kid, and a wrestler in the winter, claims they were never able to knock him over.

The other thing some seniors liked to do was single out a sophomore and dog pile them. The seniors would look for a sheep that got separated from the pack and pounce. There was no avoiding it. A couple seniors would tackle the rookie sheep and they all would pile on. Usually not a big deal. No one got hurt doing this, that year. As far as I remember, we all got it at least once and some more than once. I tried to stay with the pack for these 10 minutes or so. Others reminded me we also stayed close to the cornfields that surrounded the practice field. So like water buffalo of the Serengeti, us sophomores would try to stay in a pack, and stay near the safety of the corn field. The hovering Lions (seniors) had ten minutes to try to separate one of us. Some seniors enjoyed this old ritual more than others.

When I contacted (sophomore) Mike Opatz about this book, I asked what his memories of the season were. "That was a long time ago, but one thing I remember was that Goddamn Dizzy Dan spearing me in the back on the way to the practice field. I thought I was paralyzed. Put that in your fucking book." Dizzy Dan is Dan Bieniek. Everyone called him Dizzy Dan then. But nowadays he prefers just Dan.

This was "normal hazing" back in the 1980s. This was something that happened on the way to the practice field. Mike must have gotten separated from the pack, I don't remember this incident, but Mike remembers it vividly. Apparently, it was such a vicious hit that one of the captains, Brian Reis, even told Dan Bieniek to knock that shit off.... Incidentally, I had been pronouncing Opatz, like O-pots for thirty years or so. Until one time in the 2000s, I said O-pots, and one the boys said its O-pats. I wondered, why haven't any of those guys corrected me in the last 30 years.

Eugene Ostendorf recalled the hazing as being pretty bad. He said they surrounded him and were knocking him around back and forth. He claimed it was so bad he almost quit. I don't remember that but he loved playing football, so for him to consider quitting the hazing may have been rougher for him.

Dan Sobieck recalls when he was a rookie, one of the seniors grabbed him by the facemask and kneed him in the groin. That is just being a jackass. Some did take hazing too far and crossed the line. A few years later during a dog pile event someone did break a leg or arm or something and that put a damper on the hazing ritual.

During those first couple weeks of practices in August, before the first game, we played some scrimmages against other schools. These are informal scrimmages with full pads. Ron Fiedler reminded me of this fact when I spoke to him. We had a four-team scrimmage sometime in August before school even started. Coach Roebuck had organized this scrimmage as a way to assess the teams progress against other teams. It was not run like a game. It was just running plays. Basically, practicing plays against another team instead of against your second team at your own practice. I don't remember many details of this scrimmage but according to teammates we did pretty well. The thing is there were some bigger schools there. We held our own against these bigger schools. That was a good omen. And according to Ron Fiedler he made a prediction based on our performance there. He told Coach Roebuck that we were going to win the state title that year.

STORY ALERT - LIFE IN THE 80s

I don't remember exactly which year this happened. But it was sometime in the early 80s. During the summer before football practice had ever started, we were always looking for ways to stave off boredom. Occasionally, some friends and I like Jim Viehauser would go to the cemetery and shoot gophers. The cemetery was about three to four blocks outside of the town. We thought we were doing good and controlling the population of the nasty rodents that lived amongst the dead. At the time, it was perfectly normal to drive around the cemetery and shoot gophers. It simply was not a big deal. Our search for rodents led us to the practice fields around the school. Again, perfectly normal in the summer in the 1980s to walk around with a 22-caliber gun and shoot gophers around the school practice fields. If someone was cutting grass we wouldn't stop. But usually on weekends, in the summer there was no-one around. Gophers dug holes in the ground in the practice field, so we were simply doing our part to save players from hurting ankles.

One summer there must have been a new teacher at the school. And as Jim and I had done this before, we were on our usual route. This time I was driving and Jim was riding shotgun so to speak. Technically, this time we both had shotguns. And I was still driving with my shotgun in the front seat with me. As luck would have it—not luck for the gopher—there was a gopher on my side of the car. I had my black 1965 Pontiac Catalina. With my foot still on the gas and both hands on the shotgun I started shooting out the driver side window. It was a pump action shotgun; normally I am right-handed. But as I was driving, I had to lean out the left side and shoot left-handed. The car was moving and the gopher was moving, and for a bit no one was steering, as I shot several shots. Jim, being the good friend and loyal companion, grabbed the steering wheel with his left hand, from the passenger side and began to steer. From his vantage point, he didn't have a clear view of the gopher. So as the gopher was scootering right and left to get away, I was yelling at Jim to go left and right as well so I could get a better shot.

Now, if you can picture yourself as a new teacher at the school looking out the window, and not being familiar with typical occurrences of small-town Minnesota. You would see, on school grounds, 400 -500 yards from the school building, a big old 4 door black car with a shotgun stuck out the window, the car jerking along right and left through a grassy practice field, and then see the driver shoot five times... it might make one wonder what is going on.

Jim and I were laughing pretty hard at this point. If I remember correctly, the gopher made his escape into his hole, and as the gun only held five shells, it was empty. Even though we had shot gophers on the school grounds before, we usually dismounted and walked around the area. Shooting from a moving car, in broad daylight, on school grounds, even for us was pushing the norms a titch. Since the gun was empty, I grabbed the wheel, straightened the car out and headed for the exit. I remember seeing in the rear-view mirror, someone running out of the school, wildly waving their hands over their head. But since we were near the road and not knowing for sure if he was trying to get my attention, or if there was someone else out there doing crazy stuff, whom he wanted to speak with, I just kept driving.

Chapter 4 – Games

Coach Roebuck was meticulous in all areas. That included pre game rituals. Before home games everyone got ready and dressed early. Before we went out to the field, he had all the players sit in the darkened Little Theatre. That was the theatre area in the school where all the plays were held. We were instructed to go there and be silent while we thought about our jobs during the game. He wanted us to get focused on the game. Then he would come in and give us the pre-game pep talk.

Then we headed outside and lined up in one long line. Even our entry to the field was choreographed by the Coach. We jogged onto the field to line up for warmups. We had counted out and so as the first guy hit about the 40-yard line, every 10th player or so turned to the left and formed a line on the white field lines. So, it appeared like all the rows of ten formed five lines all at the same time. It looked kind of cool.

Week 1

Every team in the conference had high hopes for the season. The Holdingford Huskers in 1981 were no exception. The previous two seasons Holdingford had won the Central Minnesota Conference. And this team was bringing back a lot of starters from the year earlier. But this year there was some expectation that Holdingford might be bigger and better than last year. An article in the *St. Cloud Times*, on September 3rd, 1981, stated the conference race would be for second, as Holdingford was expected to win a third conference title in a row.

But you still have to play the games and anything can happen in a Friday night high school football game. There can be nerves, there can be mistakes, and as we'll see in a later game there might be an "accidental" muddy field.

The season in 1981 opened in Long Prairie on September 4th as a non-conference game. Usually, each team starts the season with a couple non-conference games before playing all the other teams in the conference. We easily won our first game by a score of 35-6. The defense gave up a touchdown in the 4th quarter. It was probably the 2nd string defense. (I don't remember.) The Husker defense would only give up 1 more touchdown, throughout the remainder of conference play.

Coach Roebuck was quoted in the Enterprise, stating: "We were basically satisfied with this first game but we've got an awful lot of improving to do before we can call ourselves a good football team."

What stands out to me is that Long Prairie had a total of 112 yards and 62 of those yards came in the 4th quarter on the long touchdown run by Randy Mechles. The defense played well. Another interesting note is that our top 2 running backs both had more rushing yards than Long Prairie had in total yards. Brian Reis, the starting halfback had 163 on 15 carries. And Dan Stich, the starting fullback, had 145 yards on 12 attempts. They each scored twice. Ron Fiedler also scored on a pass from quarterback Dale Mehr.

The game may have been a little sloppy according to Coach Roebuck, but the Huskers were quite productive.

As a sophomore on the team, I was excited to be on the sideline. I got my playing time in JV games. We had a weekly game where we got to play against the other JV teams in the conference. If we got to play in the varsity games, it was an added bonus. After the first string got way ahead, the second string got to go in. And if they didn't screw things up too badly, Coach Roebuck sent us third stringers in to run a few plays. Coach Roebuck's son, Jeff was also a sophomore. So, it seems he wanted to get us Sophomores in to run a few plays in each varsity game. I was a wide receiver and we always ran running plays. Always. I don't recall us third stringers ever calling a pass play. We would usually run three plays and very rarely, if ever, get a first down and then we would punt. The first team would give us some good-natured ribbing for not moving the ball.

And now the team was 1-0. The Huskers gained 347 rushing yards in the first game. Mostly Brian Reis and Dan Stich. Some people realized these running backs, Brian Reis and Dan Stich, may be special. I don't recall it was something that was talked about yet. This was just the beginning of what would be an amazing year for both of them.

Week 2

The second game of the year was against another non-conference team. The Pierz Pioneers. Neither team scored in the first quarter but the gates opened in the second quarter when Brian Reis and Dan Stich both scored. In the 3rd quarter our quarterback, Dale Mehr ran for his first, second, and third touchdowns of the season. Holdingford won 33-0. Holdingford gained almost 400 yards in the game. 379 of those yards came from rushing. The mighty Huskers were 2-0. These were non-conference games, and our first test would be the following Friday night, against a solid Sartell Sabres team who was a rival of the Huskers, and who were expected to be fighting for the second position in the conference.

Week 3

Our third game was against conference rival Sartell. The teams in the conference were determined by the size of the school. Based on students per grade. The teams we played in the conference, Sartell, St John's Prep, Kimball, Maple Lake, Eden Valley-Watkins, Becker, and Big Lake, were all about the same size. A lot of these teams we had played against for many years.

There were great rivalries in our conference. Holdingford was certainly a rural school, like Eden Valley and Kimball. Sartell was more of a suburb of the bigger city of St. Cloud. If one wanted to group the schools into a demographic, we would have been considered the farm kids and Sartell would have been considered the city kids. It was especially fun to beat them down year after year. There was no serious dislike of any teams, but only friendly competition. In my experience, if any team was dirty, it was Kimball. In 1981 we beat them badly. But in the JV game, they beat us. They had a strong sophomore class of athletes. They just didn't play with class. We play to play and we win or we lose. It is OK to lose, the joy was in playing. But they were cheap and dirty. When you play for a Coach like Coach Roebuck, you know the difference between classy and dirty.

Sartell was classy. We still had a rivalry and we wanted to win. So did they. At this point in the year, Holdingford was ranked second in the state in Class B. Sartell was ranked tenth. (Mahnomen, our arch nemesis was ranked first.)

The mighty Huskers "crushed" (per the *St. Cloud Times*) the Sartell Sabres, 28-0. Brian Reis had a big game with 184 yards of total offense. He rushed, he caught passes, he returned punts and intercepted a pass. He scored twice. Dale Mehr and Ron Fiedler each scored once. And in the fourth quarter defensive end, big Jim Ertl (Doc) tackled Sartell in the endzone to get a safety. Coach Roebuck was quoted by the St Cloud Times: "I think that we're further along this year, at this point of the season, than at any time I can remember. But that doesn't count now. We still have to gel at the end of the season. And we have to bounce back off this one and play another undefeated team [St. John's Prep] next week." Coach Roebuck knew this team was special but he also knew the team needed to keep up the intensity and constantly work on slight improvement each week. The goal would be to peak at the end of the year and not in the middle of the season.

The Huskers were 3-0 and had only given up one touchdown on the season.

Week 4

Game four was against St. John's prep. They were also 3-0. St John's is a prep school on the grounds of the famous St. John's University. In 1981, St. John's University was coached by another coaching legend, John Gagliardi. He coached in Collegeville, Minnesota for 60 years. When he died in 2018, according to the *St. Paul*

Pioneer Press, he had more football wins than any college coach in history, with 489 victories.

On the campus was a school for high school-aged kids. They were in the central Minnesota conference and we played them every year for many years. Since both teams were undefeated at the time, one might think it to be a close game. Not at all. The rolling Huskers won 43-7. It was never close as the Huskers gained 442 yards. St. John's did score, and it was only the second touchdown the stout Huskers defense had given up all year. It would be the last until the playoffs.

Allan Reis opened the scoring in this game with a field goal. We scored early and often. Dan Stich scored a couple touchdowns. Tight end Ron Pierskalla scored twice in this game. Brian Reis scored by way of punt return. And reserve running back Dan Koehn scored a touchdown late in the 4th quarter.

St. John's Prep coach Pete Cheeley summed up his feelings about the Huskers in the St. Cloud Times: "A team like Holdingford is going to turn mistakes into points. I'll say this, and you can quote me, I'm glad we don't have to play them again. (Until the following year, when they ended our own 14 game win streak.) Cheeley's goal was to slow down Brian Reis and they held him to 124 yards on 10 carries. But their focus on Reis opened up opportunities for Dan Stich and the passing game, which Coach Roebuck took advantage of. Coach Cheeley did pay Reis and the offense a compliment in a CMS article by Dale Stonehouse: "We wanted to stop their option defensively, but we never shut anything down. We tried to stop Reis, but I don't know if he can be stopped. He's a fabulous back."

Coach Roebuck in the Enterprise gave credit to the front line for the 379 yards of offensive production: "Much of that was possible by the efforts of Holdingford's offensive line, consisting of Mark Nentl, Jim Ertl, Brian Danzl, Scott Yurczyk, Allan Reis, Dean Sowada, and Ron Pierskalla."

The undefeated and untested Huskers were 4-0.

This game was played in Holdingford and was our Homecoming game. Homecoming week was a big event for the school. Each day of the week had a designated theme. Like wearing green one day. Wear a hat one day. Dress up in a costume one day. Then it all culminated in a pep rally on Friday before the big game. As Mark Nentl pointed out, the cheerleaders put a lot of extra time and effort into supporting the team. We did have other pep rallies before some of the games that year. For one of the skits, the cheerleaders brought out about 5 of the seniors and sat them on a chair and blindfolded them. They explained that one of the cheerleaders would kiss them and they had to guess which cheerleader it was. Great idea, sounds like fun. After the blindfolds were on however, the five players' moms came out from behind the curtain. The students in the stands loved it. The moms kissed their sons and the players had to guess, which they all tried to do, to hoots and hollers of the students. After they all guessed, they removed their blindfolds and saw their moms standing there. The crowd appreciated the show.

Week 5

On October 2nd, we played against another conference rival, Kimball. The Huskers steamrolled over the Kimball Cubs by gaining 455 in total offensive yards. Dan Stich and Brian Reis both scored with Stich getting two, and Reis getting three. Even the second stringers got in on the action with Greg Konsor passing to Ron Lehner for a score in the 4th quarter. Which means us third stringers might've played as well. The Husker defense held the Kimball team to 68 yards of total offense. This was an impressive win for the Huskers, dominating on offense and defense.

With a win of 39-0, the red hot Holdingford Huskers were 5-0.

Two years later, in 1983, the Kimball Cubs team went undefeated in the conference and moved on to play in the postseason; they lost in the playoffs. I remember this very well because I was a senior that year and we were 8-1 and our one loss was to Kimball, so they got the playoff spot for our Conference.

Week 6

October 9th 1981, The Maple Lake Irish came to Holdingford as the number two team in the Conference and they were also undefeated. Sounds like a set up for a very exciting match up. Not to be. Once again, the promised drama never manifested. The Irish had no luck that Friday night. By the end of the first quarter the Huskers were ahead 22-0 and the Irish luck never improved. The final score was 48-0. The Huskers scored 7 rushing touchdowns in the first three quarters. Dan Stich, Brian Reis, Dale Mehr all rushed for two touchdowns and Ron "a lot of Dan's and none worth a damn" Fiedler also ran one in. The Hardy Huskers were now 6-0.

There were still 3 conference games left, and people around the area could feel the excitement in the air. This team was special. We were simply destroying previously unbeaten teams. We were racking up 300-400 yards per game on the ground. The defense was holding opposing teams to under 100 yards per game. We had only given up two touchdowns all year. On top of the outstanding defense, the offense was unstoppable. Brian Reis was averaging somewhere around ten yards per carry. Which meant he averaged a first down every time he touched the ball. Dan Stich was right there with him. They were both getting multiple scores per game.

Coach Roebuck was not one to look ahead. Even with all the excitement and the press from the local papers, Coach Roebuck always took it one game at a time. In practice the team would work on things needing improvement. One could argue if we gained 400 yards a game, what do we need to improve on? In speaking with the players for this book, they mentioned that he was always working on technique with the linemen. He had the talent to picture each player and automatically assess where they were and where they could be. He wanted to improve each player to go up a step in skill each game. He would get them to do a little better or be a little more effective each week. And each player has a different personality and learns differently. Some need a firm touch, while others retract from the firm approach and need and respond to the soft approach. Coach Roebuck possessed the incredibly subtle ability to know how much he could push someone and also know how to not push them too far.

That applied to conditioning, too. We were dominating the conference teams, but we always had heavy conditioning in practice. Our conditioning was not for the next three games. It was for the teams we would meet in the playoffs. Then we would play teams who were the best in their respective conferences. The games would likely be harder and closer. I firmly believe the conditioning we did in August, September, and October was for the games we would play in November. And I also contend the conditioning we did throughout the year was because Coach Roebuck knew we would likely have to get through Mahnomen at some point. They had beaten us the previous two years. The coach knew they were big and strong, and very evenly matched to us talent wise.

Even though we just won a game 48-0, we ran sprints and fourth quarter drills during the next week of practice. They were not a punishment, so one could describe them as Fitness Insurance for the future. Running and sweating aren't bad for you. Though they may not be fun at the time, there are certainly benefits to running. We continued to condition during practice.

Which does bring up a memory from the following year. In 1982 our team was 4-5. We simply weren't a very good team. I specifically remember a time during the year when we were not doing well. It was during a speech session about the season. The subject of conditioning came up, and win or lose we were going to continue to run sprints and fourth quarter drills. The Coach said something like, "We will be the best conditioned average team around." He believed in conditioning, win or lose, because sometimes when you need just a little extra to win, and maybe it's in the fourth quarter, and just maybe that extra energy is the difference in a big win. In November of 1981, that may have been the difference that made for a perfect season.

Week 7

We faced Eden Valley in our next game.

While doing research for this story, I heard this rumor: Someone at Eden Valley accidently left the sprinklers on the night before this game, and the field was basically a swamp. Remember in the movie Bull Durham where Kevin Costner's character wanted a day off, so they turned the sprinklers on the baseball field and the game was called off? Well in football, if the field is muddy, you don't take the game off. You play the game on a muddy field. And that is what happened. There were rumors that this may not have been an accident, but a way to hopefully slow down the potent Huskers offense. It didn't work. We did only win 27-0, and one could speculate that the muddy field kept the score down. Dan Stich scored first on the opening kickoff with an 80-yard touchdown return. Brian Reis scored 3 more touchdowns and still had 183 total yards on the wet and slippery field.

This is just my opinion but speaking from experience playing on a muddy field is more fun. You get all dirty and footing is tricky but the field is softer when you get tackled. Your uniform is all muddy and you feel you are more productive, than if your clothes are still clean after a game.

The muddy-uniformed Huskers were 7-0.

Week 8

The Becker squad, our eighth week's opponent, was 4-3. The Huskers at this point looked unstoppable, so no matter how much you try to motivate your team of young players in Becker, even they knew the team from Holdingford was the real deal. The Huskers were regularly racking up over 300 yards per game and generally giving up under 100 yards per game. There was a quote in the St. Cloud Times from Becker's head coach, Dwight Lundeen. Coach Lundeen said, likely partially in jest, "I'm praying for a lot of snow, a frozen field, or a lot of anything the Lord would like to send." Well, it seems the Good Lord was a fan of the Mighty Green Machine this week. Holdingford (school colors green and white) won this match up 38-0.

Coach Lundeen also said wishfully, "We're going to try to contain that great Holdingford backfield," meaning Brian Reis and Dan Stich. Easier said than done. Reis scored three touchdowns on runs of 56, 52, and 83 yards. Stich added 2 touchdown runs. Brian Reis broke a Holdingford school record by gaining 308 yards on 16 carries. The humble Reis was quick to give all the credit to the Holdingford linemen. He mentioned they opened the holes and were with him down the field as well. Dan Stich gained 151 yards on 13 carries. There was no containing Holdingford's backfield. You could try different schemes but our duo of explosive running backs were eventually going to break out.

The unblemished Huskers were 8-0.

Week 9

On October 30th, the Huskers played their final game of the regular season against Big Lake. The win was never in doubt as the Big Green Machine rolled over Big Lake 27-0. Stich and Reis both scored as did the wingback Ron Fiedler. Junior Steve Barrett capped the scoring with a 19-yard interception return for a touchdown. Perhaps another reason this wasn't a high scoring game is because Coach Roebuck knew there were some Mahnomen scouts in attendance. He didn't run motion plays or some other of our effective plays. He didn't want to show them too much. The yet-to-be-tested

Holdingford Huskers ended the regular season with a perfect record of 9-0.

The regular season was completed. The Huskers team did what they set out to do months before. As a team you set incremental goals. Take each game one at a time with the goal to win. The goal in each game is to score as many touchdowns as possible and to give up as few as possible to the opposing team. The team scored a lot of touchdowns and only gave up two in these first 9 games. Doing that allows you to accomplish the next goal which is to make the playoffs. We had done that. We had more goals for the year, and the first huge step was complete. We were in the playoffs and ranked 2nd in the state, still behind Mahnomen who was number 1, and also undefeated.

Speaking of those 2 touchdowns, brings up another story. The first touchdown the Huskers gave up was in the first game of the year against Long Prairie in a non-conference game. It happened in the 4th quarter on a long run. The second-string defense was probably in and since it was a non-conference game that touchdown is forgiven and forgotten.

However, thirty years after the 1981 season, Holdingford did a tribute to the team at one of the high school football games. The coaches and many players were there. As I did research on this book, I was chatting with Jim Ertl, who has the best memory of any player I spoke with. He remembers a lot of details for the season that occurred 40 years ago. He was telling me that while speaking with Dan Stich at the thirty-year reunion of the championship, Dan Stich was still upset about the touchdown St. John's scored in their game. Dan Stich, a farmer's son, was by most accounts the toughest guy on the team. He was not the tallest or biggest. But he was fast and strong. The program listed him at 170 lbs. And he loved hitting people during the game. A quarter of a century later he was still upset about that score.

      Forty years later, I asked him about the score to get clarification. Was he upset and why? What he told me speaks volumes about his personality on the field. He explained that the goal of every game was a shutout and to give up less than 100 yards in total offense, which the team did a lot that year. According to him, we were ahead 24-0 in the second quarter. This was Holdingford's Homecoming game and most likely Coach Roebuck wanted to get more players in, so with the game in hand, he substituted in a lot of others players on defense. St. Johns was driving the ball and as they got close to the goal line, the first-string defense went back in. However, St. John's did manage to score a touchdown, on a 4-yard run by quarterback Paul Larson. Stich does not blame the 2nd stringers as the first team was on the field when it happened. There was a rumor that he may have missed a tackle that allowed them to score. I hesitantly inquired about that. His response via text was: "By the way, I did not miss tackles." He had the linebacker mentality of a Jack Lambert or a Mike Singletary. In 12 games the team did record 9 shutouts.

Dan Stich had every quality of a great football player. But he also had the football instincts to always be where the ball runner was. At the end of the season, he was named all-conference linebacker, in a unanimous decision; every coach in the conference said he was the best linebacker in the conference. That is high praise. And he was also an all-conference fullback. He was first team all-conference on offense and defense.

Many of the starters on offense also started on defense. Three juniors: Lee Odden, Scott Volkers, and Ron Pierskalla started on defense.

Actually, there were several players that year who were all-conference: Dale Mehr, Brian Reis, Brian Danzl, Jim Ertl, Mark Nentl, and others. Some were for both offense and defense.

During the season it wasn't all serious. Some players mentioned that in the huddles there were some jokes. These players had been playing football together for years. They were friends.

Mark Nentl brought up a story. It was during a game when Holdingford was way ahead. The Huskers were just flagged for a penalty and it was something like 3rd and 20 or 25 on their own 40-yard line. The Coach sent in the play. He said run whatever you want. He figured they would just run the ball and punt the next play. Well, Nentl had a feeling, and he said let's do "36 belly." Quarterback Dale Mehr looked back over his shoulder and said OK. Mark wanted to run this play because the ball was to go to Brian Reis and he was to make the key block at the line. His feeling was correct and Brian scored on a 60-yard run. In the endzone Brian handed Mark the ball in an acknowledgement of a good call. Since you can't spike the ball in high school, Mark just gave the ball to the ref.

STORY ALERT - LIFE IN THE 80s

Holdingford was a small enough town where nothing really crazy happened. People left doors open. Kids walked back and forth to school safely. Sixteen-year-old kids got their driver's license and were pretty good and safe drivers. Fifteen-year-old kids on the farm already had a farm permit. Not that it mattered. I remember driving our farm truck to the fields when I was nine or ten years old.

My recollection is the worst thing kids did was drink beers on weekends. In high school, I don't remember ever seeing any drugs. Just cheap beer like Pfeiffer's, and Cold Spring beer. Or cheap wine like Mad Dog 2020 and cheap hard liquor occasionally. I remember an instance once in the summer when we were about 14. It was late June or July. My parents were away and for the first time I remember they left my seventeen-year-old brother Steve and me alone in our house. It was for maybe two nights.

Well not to miss an opportunity, I had four friends over and we were splitting a case of beer. At about midnight I had the great idea of blowing off some fireworks. We walked about one block to the large playground at the Elementary school. I had some cool bottle rockets and other noise-making fireworks. Remember it was about midnight. Well after a few minutes of this fireworks show, and us obviously forgetting that we had a cop in town, the cop car shows up. We decided running in the opposite direction would be a good idea. A couple of us ended up in someone's yard, (Currently the Waletzko's), hiding around their house. The cop drove around the area, and I made my escape home. Eugene Ostendorf at the wrong time in the wrong place climbed over the wrong fence, and ended up right in front of the police. They were small town cops and this wouldn't turn into an international incident. They most likely just wanted to scare us. Incidentally, one of the town cops was my cousin, and he had recognized me, and when they "interrogated" Eugene Ostendorf, he cracked within seconds. By then I had made my way home. I hid the remainder of the beer case in the tub.

Then, since the universe has a sense of humor, two interesting and probably expected things occurred. Funny now, but not funny or interesting at the time. There was a knock at the door and the phone rang. I answered the door and my brother answered the phone. At the door were the two cops... On the phone was my mom, asking how things were going? The phone and the main door were in our kitchen. My brother Steve is talking to my mom on the phone while watching me talk to the cops 10 feet away. Fortunately, he stayed quiet about the cop visit.

At the door the police took me outside and went through the deserved scare tactic. They explained why fireworks at midnight are bad. Why running from the police is bad. And why having illegal fireworks is bad. (The fireworks I had come from Wisconsin, where they are legal, but were illegal in Minnesota.) So, they told me to go inside and grab all the illegal fireworks. I gave them about half of what I had. I was sure he wouldn't search my room. My fourteen-year-old brain had it all figured out. He confiscated them and gave me a stern warning. Just as an example, that is one of the crazier things I did as a teenager. Pretty mild and tame compared to nowadays. My parents never found out. As far as I know.

Chapter 5 – Playoffs

I don't know what it was like in other communities but Holdingford was a very serious Catholic community. In fact, when I was a freshman at Mankato State University a few years later, I was in a geography class and the professor was talking about immigration and religion in Minnesota. He was talking about some towns that were Swedish and Lutheran and Polish or German and Catholic, and he specifically mentioned Holdingford as a community that was over 90% Catholic. For me that was normal but apparently that statistic is a bit unusual. Anyway, as we got into the playoffs that year, the church held a special mass for the players before the games. The mass was on Thursday after practice. Someone brought a football and the priest blessed it and the players and asked the Good Lord for good fortune for the team. It was open to the community and was optional for everyone. All this was normal to us as an overwhelmingly Catholic community. A mass occurred before each of the next three games. I am not sure how the mass was organized or by whom. Coach Roebuck was not Catholic. So, I don't know if he was involved. As I mentioned going to the mass was optional and it happened after school and after football practice. It was somehow organized by the community. In 1981 it was a perfectly normal thing to happen in Holdingford, and a lot of players went to it.

The Green Machine of Holdingford finished the regular season 9-0, with 7 shutouts. And the defense only gave up 2 touchdowns the entire year. The team, as they say, was firing on all cylinders. No one was making room in the trophy case yet, however. Everyone knew we had at least 3 more games to play. And one of those games would likely be against the juggernaut Mahnomen. Mahnomen was the Achilles heel of Gary Roebuck and the Holdingford Huskers. Mahnomen would be our Mt. Everest, something we would have to conquer before we could lift the state title trophy over our heads.

Coach Roebuck knew that the road to a state title went through Mahnomen. We were fast and talented, and they were bigger and had won the state title the previous year. In the previous two years we had won our conference and both years ended when the team ran into the buzz saw that was Mahnomen. Mahnomen was at the time on a twenty-three-game winning streak.

But first we had to play the Pierz Pioneers in the opening round of the playoffs. We had faced them a couple months earlier in a non-conference game. That game we won 33-0. They won their conference and their reward was a rematch against the number 2 ranked

Huskers. The Pioneers had a young team that year, with a lot of sophomores making up their starting roster. Their coach, Steve Dooley, tried to maintain an optimistic attitude. In a *St. Cloud Times* article by Mike Killeen, Coach Dooley stated: "We've seen our sophomores develop. We were a bunch of young kids and we hope we improved with the year's experience. If we've improved 33 points, though, I don't know." They may in fact have improved, but so did we.

Brian Reis scored touchdowns the first 3 times he touched the ball, on runs of 70, 61, and 64 yards. Bill Shank reflected that often during the year, our offense was so good when we showed up, the other team was intimidated. Imagine you are a Pierz player and they watch the All-State running back Reis, score 3 touchdowns on 3 carries. Your team is down by 3 touchdowns and you have yet to tackle the guy. I believe that would deflate your optimism. He ended the first half with 4 touchdown runs. He didn't play offense much in the second half as the game was well in hand. He finished the game with 273 yards on 6 carries. (That is 45.5 yards per carry, if you are keeping track.) He also caught 2 passes for 44 yards. Interestingly, Reis touched the ball 8 times offensively, but was only tackled 4 times. Ron Fiedler and Ron Pierskalla each scored on passes from Dale Mehr. Holdingford dominated the Pioneers and won 41-0. Holdingford did fumble the ball 3 times, which was a bad omen leading up to the next game.

In a *St. Cloud Times* article, written by Mike Schroeder, the Pierz Coach Dooley summed up the Huskers squad: "Holdingford is just an awesome club. I think it's in the cards for them this year. Their kids are such a unit, and they work so well together. You look at Reis, but they have some good kids on the line too—you've got to give them credit. "

That line he was referring to had senior Brian Danzl at center. On one side was senior guard Jim Ertl and senior tackle Mark Nentl. The tight end was one of two junior starters, Ron Pierskalla. On the other side were two players who rotated on each play and brought the plays in, seniors Scott Yurczyk and Dean Sowada, at guard. The other starting junior was Allan Reis at tackle, who is the 190 lbs little brother to Brian Reis.

Coach Roebuck was also generous in his praise of the offensive line. He knew the credit for opening holes went to the front line. Brian Reis and Dan Stich had their names in the paper each week because they scored a lot of touchdowns, someone had to open the holes for them. And that was this excellent front line.

When Brian Reis broke the school record for yards in a game with 308, against Becker earlier in the season, he was quick to give credit to the line. In a *St. Cloud Times* article by Mike Schroeder, Reis stated: "The line is about the quickest we've ever had. They got downfield and sealed off really well. It seemed like Brian Danzl was downfield all night long either leading me or right behind me."

In a separate *Times* article by Mike Schroeder before the Mahnomen game, he devoted the whole story to the Holdingford Huskers front line. He names all the starters and claims they: "Form what may be the best offensive line in Central Minnesota, and possibly, one of the top contingents in Minnesota." No argument from me.

I think Mehr, Reis, and Stich would agree we had a fantastic line who opened holes for the running backs to run through. In conference play, they dominated. They may have been undersized, but when you factor in heart and discipline, they were perfect.

Mark Nentl was the biggest player on the team at 240 lbs and played strong-side tackle. He was also a heavyweight wrestler in the winter which certainly helped him as a lineman. He was strong and efficient. Next to him at guard was Jim Ertl who was tall and farm-kid strong and wanted to play every play.

Junior Allen Reis was the strongest kid on the team and was the tackle on the other side and he was also the kicker.

Brain Danzl was listed at 175 lbs and started at center and as a tackle on defense. He played well above his weight and he was fast for a lineman. As Reis stated, he was often down field looking for someone else to hit. Coach Roman Pierskalla worked a lot with the defense and also coached Brian Danzl in wrestling. He said Danzl was one of the toughest guys on the team.

Scott Yurczyk at 150 lbs rotated in with Dean Sowada at 165 lbs at the other guard position. They may seem light for a guard but they were players who gained Coach Roebucks confidence by being quick and efficient and skillful in their position.

As mentioned, the line certainly did well during all the previous games. The challenge for Coach Roebuck was the next game against Mahnomen. The size of the line was pretty comparable to all the teams in our conference. However, they were slightly smaller and lighter compared to the Mahnomen linemen. The previous year, the Mahnomen Indians beat Holdingford 23-0 in the semi-final game. The Coach was quoted as saying we got beat in the trenches in that game.

I do remember during the week before the game against Mahnomen, Coach Roebuck gave us a pep talk. He combined all the weight of the players on the line and divided that by the 5-6 players on the line and came up with an average weight. He did the same with the Mahnomen team. With the average we only came in at 10-20 lbs lighter per person. Now, if you are a mathematician, you will realize that when you factor in Mark Nentl at 240 lbs, it brings the average up for all the lineman. Because some of their linemen were more than 20 lbs heavier than some of our linemen, I believe it was a psychological attempt to help boost the confidence of the lineman. He might have said he was using creative numbers and actual statistics, which he was. I believe it worked. (Coach Bruns also noted that occasionally Coach Roebuck would use a creative numbering system when calculating the players weight, height and 40-yard dash speed.) Anyway, Coach Roebuck knew there would be a battle at the line of scrimmage. He was right, and looking back when it was all over, the line did a remarkable job tangling with the Mahnomen team.

That leads us to the game of the century, at least for us farm kids.

STORY ALERT - LIFE IN THE 80s

Tim Brown brought this story up. This occurred in the summer of a later year, though. We were at a party at his cabin in the woods. We somehow thought it would be a good idea to put a couch on the roof of the cabin. It wouldn't sit flat as it was on the peak. So, you could rock it a little. Problem was if you rocked it too much back, it could topple over backwards. Let's not get into the philosophical debate of why kids might think this was a good idea, or even a logical thing to do. It is not a good idea, and it is not logical. I always defer to the answer that we were young and dumb. And hey, teenage brains aren't fully developed.

Well guess what happened, to the surprise of no one, Tim Brown and I were on the couch and it went a little too far backwards... and over we went. Now to the people in the front of the cabin, all they saw was the couch tilt backward, and our legs and feet go up and over the top, and out of sight. May have looked scary even if they had a couple beers in them. Well, the good news is there was enough roof on the back side, and the roof wasn't very steep, that we were able to stay on the roof and not slide off to the ground, which wouldn't have been fun. Though it was only an 8–10-foot drop. We thought this was pretty funny. Again, our brains were not fully developed.

Chapter 6 – Mahnomen

I see similarities between Coach Roebuck and Coach Herb Brooks of the USA Olympic hockey team. As Herb Brooks knew the team had to get past the bigger and stronger Soviet team, so Coach Roebuck knew we'd have to get past the slightly bigger and confident Mahnomen team.

We were fast and talented but they were bigger and had won the state title the previous year. In the previous 2 years we had won the conference and both years ended when the team ran into the buzz saw that was Mahnomen. Mahnomen was at the time on a 23-game win streak. Herb Brooks focused on things he could control. One of them was conditioning. Same with coach Roebuck. I don't know if he realized how good we would be and that we would easily win through the conference games. But I suspect he did know. When we were practicing in August, we were doing wind sprints, and 4th quarter drills, which were designed to promote muscle failure, I guess. The result was that in games later in the season, when we needed an extra gear in the 4th quarter, we had an extra gear. So just as Herb Brooks pushed conditioning, because he could at least control that against the Soviets, Coach Roebuck, in similar fashion, could control that against the Mahnomen team we were likely to face in the playoffs.

As Dale Mehr reflected on the season years later, our team had yet to be tested. Of the ten wins so far, eight games were shutouts, with the two other teams each scoring one touchdown apiece. The Huskers were steam rolling and dominating their opponents.

The Mahnomen game was the semi-finals; the only thing between Holdingford and the state championship game. We easily won the next game for the state championship. In my humble opinion, the Mahnomen game was the most pivotal and exciting game ever played, before or since, by the Holdingford Huskers.

The Mahnomen Indians (now the Thunderbirds) were also a great team with a superb coach. Mahnomen coach, Ken Baumann, was in his 13th year in 1981. His career record at the time was 109-16-2. He was also accustomed to winning. For the last two years his team had beaten Holdingford in the State semi-finals. They were currently on a 23-game winning streak, capping their previous season with a state championship. Up to this point, perhaps we hadn't been tested; however, everyone knew we would be tested in this game, no one more so than Coach Roebuck. On paper we were a bit smaller. They were ranked number one in the state. We were ranked number two. Their modus operandi was domination. The game would be played on their home field.

Coach Roebuck had been preparing his team for this game since the end of the 1980 season. When we started practices in August and were doing conditioning drills, it was all related to this rematch of Class B titans. In games during the season, we could predict the result after a few minutes of football. No one knew it, but this game wouldn't be decided clearly until the final play of the game. This could've and should've been the game of the week on ESPN. It was a classic struggle between fairly equally matched teams, each coached by coaches with a propensity for winning. This game was destined to be an epic clash that is still discussed and dissected decades later in all the bars and taverns of Holdingford, and likely other parts of the state. (At least I think so.)

Even though we were 10-0, and had only given up two touchdowns all year, we were the underdogs here. That should tell you something about the reputation and quality of the Mahnomen football program. They were a somewhat bigger team. They also had a great head coach who had experience in these late season games. We did have the all state running back, and a bunch of all-conference players. What we also had, which isn't on the stat sheet, was a group of strong, scrappy, country kids with a tendency for winning football games since the 7th grade, and a never-quit attitude. Everyone expected it to be a close, hard-fought game. We thought we would win. At least we hoped we would win. However, in the 4th quarter we didn't plan on being down 14-7 with them driving toward our endzone for another score.

The game actually started out well for Holdingford. In the first quarter, the Huskers' Brian Reis scored on a 40-yard scamper. Things were looking good for the mighty Green Machine. Shortly after that, Mahnomen scored on a 12-yard run by Pete Liebl. Then in the 2nd quarter there was some miscommunication and Dale Mehr pitched the ball to the wrong side and Mahnomen picked up the loose ball and took it to the Holdingford three-yard line. A couple plays later Mahnomen scored and they were ahead 14-7. That is how the first half ended. After the game Mehr was interviewed and he spoke about that fumble: "I thought I was going to be the goat because of the pitchout, I turned the wrong way and that messed things up." Goat in that context didn't mean greatest of all time. It was the other goat. Mehr more than made up for that later in the game.

Coach Roebuck made some adjustments in the second half. In a brilliant move, he pulled the rover linebacker and added an extra defensive nose guard. That player was Dan Bieniek. Dan Gill and Scott Radtke and others also subbed in on the defensive line. As they were running the ball and moving, he wanted more people up front to help slow them down. Brilliant because as we know, Mahnomen didn't score again. No one scored in the 3rd quarter.

Now, back to the 4th quarter with Mahnomen driving. Things were looking bleak. I remember being on the sideline during this drive. If they scored another touchdown, we would have needed two touchdowns in the last seven minutes to win. The odds of that happening were slim. We needed a miracle.

Well, in the middle of the darkest minute of this game, we got a miracle. As they were driving at our about 25-yard line they called another run play. Per Coach Baumann, their quarterback Ken Muckenhirn was trying to hand the ball off to a running back. It was not a clean hand off. Per Holdingford players we had defensive linemen in their backfield disrupting the handoff. Per Dan Bieniek, in years past, he claims to have hit the quarterback. I watched the old black and white tape of the play with forty-year-old technology and I cannot discern exactly what happened. What we can see is they were trying to hand off, and we did have players disrupting the play, and the ball popped up and landed in Brian Danzl's hands, as he was certainly in their backfield.

Next thing you know, he was off in the direction of the endzone. He was fairly fast and he had an open field in front of him. A huge cheer went up on our sideline as he sprinted past. There were a few white and green jerseys trying to keep up with him, and there was one guy in the dark jersey of Mahnomen who chased after him. It was Muckenhirn who finally caught him and dragged him down at about the five-yard line. We call this the Immaculate Fumble Recovery. I mean, I call it that.

After the game Danzl was asked about the play by Times reporter Mike Schroeder: "The play was broken up before I got there," said Danzl, his uniform spotted with blood. "I saw the ball bounce and hit the ground. It's the first time I've ever had to run with a fumble." Danzl added: "I only saw that orange thing (end zone marker) down there. I thought I was going to pass out. I just didn't have it." What he did have was enough.

That play completely changed the circumstances of the game. Rather than us being down by a possible two touchdowns, we were instead about to at least tie the game. That was a pivotal play indeed. But we still had to punch it in against this sturdy defense. Two running plays were stopped. The tension was building.

Then the coach called the next play and Dale Mehr scored a touchdown on a quarterback sneak to make it 13-14.

Now Coach Roebuck had to make a gutsy decision in one of the biggest games of his career. Some coaches would kick the extra point and go for the tie, hoping for good luck in overtime.

Here is another example of the genius of Coach Roebuck. After speaking with Dale Mehr. It turns out the coach added a two-point conversion play two weeks before the game with Mahnomen. You see, in his mind, overtime was not a good option for us. Obviously, the coach had given this a lot of thought. Overtime in High School the ball is placed on the 10-yard line and each team gets four downs to score. You can score a touchdown or kick a field goal. If it is a tie, both teams go again from the ten, until someone ends up with more points after both teams get the ball. After Dale Mehr explained this to me, I now understand Coach Roebucks thinking.

Mahnomen was a bigger and perhaps more powerful team. Four downs from the ten was more in their wheelhouse. We were an open field, speed team, and we were good at breaking open long runs. With only ten yards, the overtime rules were not conducive with our strengths. Coach decided if it came down to kicking for a tie or going for two for the win, we would go for the two-point conversion, and he designed a play for that contingency.

Amazingly, that is exactly what happened. Which means Coach Roebuck is some sort of football savant. He had thought enough about all the sceneries to predict that we may need a two-point conversion play. He was right. We did. We used it.

The play was designed for Dale Mehr to fake to Dan Stich inside and then sweep out to the sideline with the intention of Dale keeping it. He had other options but Coach Roebuck told Dale he was the primary option. I do remember watching this play from the near sideline. The play was from the three-yard line. But the play ran to the far side of the field, and there was a huge collision at the goal line and was difficult to see. For a couple seconds no one on our side could tell what happened. (The next day my dad said the same thing. He was listening to the game at home on the radio. He said there was a long pause after the collision at the goal line before the referee made a signal. All who were listening, as the game was not televised back in 1981, held their collective breath until the radio broadcaster announced the call.)

Then the referee put both hands up to signify a successful conversion. Our sideline exploded with excitement as the high-risk play worked and we were ahead 15-14, late in the game.

After the game Coach Roebuck was quoted in the *St. Cloud Times*: "We practiced that play every day for the last two weeks. We knew that if the game went into overtime, we'd have a hard time stopping their big runners. There was no question that we were going for it." Dale Mehr echoed that sentiment as he stated: "We knew we'd go for two as soon as we scored (the touchdown). "Once I got outside, I figured if I dove, I could make it."

We were ahead but there were still seven minutes to go in the game. All we had to do was hold them. Which is easy to say but hard to do, as they were a powerful team with a winning personality.

However, when I rewatched the finals minutes of this game for this book, the Huskers defense played like demons possessed. They tasted blood in the water and Mahnomen could not move the ball. Picture a momma bear protecting her cubs, as that was the Huskers defense protecting midfield. In those last several minutes, Mahnomen had the ball three times and punted twice and lost the ball on downs with about one minute to go. I believe they never crossed midfield in those final minutes.

We ended up with the ball with about 1 minute to go in the game. Brian Reis broke free and scored another touchdown. We missed the extra point. Now it was 21-14. That could have been a disaster as Mahnomen had one more opportunity with forty-one seconds to play. Fortunately, the stout Huskers defense held them and sacked their quarterback, for the final play as the last second ticked to zero.

This is where I wish I was a better writer. I am a storyteller, and a tad bit of a bull shitter at times, but if I was a better writer, I could somehow capture the epicness and excitement of this game. To somehow convey how monumental, it was for this group of farm and country kids to go into Mahnomen and stop the reigning state champs, and end their twenty-three-game win streak. I will do my best. We had hundreds of fans at this game. This game was epic. This game was the culmination for Coach Roebuck of many years of coaching. This was him conquering his Mount Everest. This was his best team in all those years of coaching, so if we didn't win here, one could wonder how we could ever win it all. As Mark Petron told me, that season was his masterpiece, which would make this game the central theme to the masterpiece.

Our sideline erupted with full-fledged jubilation. The field filled with ecstatic Holdingford fans.

The fans who witnessed the game knew this was an amazing achievement. There was still one more game to go, but beating Mahnomen was like conquering Mt. Everest. The Holdingford players, with their backs against the wall in the 4th quarter, never quit. Things were looking dire with only minutes to go in the game. But even as the Mahnomen team was driving, all eleven players on the field kept fighting. Coach Roebuck often stressed during practice individual players doing their specific job, and when they all did that, good things would happen.

It was a great achievement but after the game the coach stressed there was still one more game to play. Hold onto that intensity.

On the bus after the game, Scott Lange was sitting behind Roebuck and Bruns. He overheard them talking. Coach Roebuck said something like, "We certainly didn't overpower them. We out finessed them." Scott recently shared this comment with me. This is a really telling statement. We were undefeated and a great team. But Mahnomen was also a great team, with more championship game experience, and they were fairly strong, and bigger. This comment appears to imply that he knew we had to finesse them. We weren't going to push them around. We weren't going to dominate them, like we had in the other ten games that season. His strategy had worked.

An article in the Times also mentioned that the Huskers out maneuvered the Mahnomen team.

I don't know if one can plan for luck. But I know one can plan for endurance. We won this game because of events that occurred late in the 4th quarter with under eight minutes to go in the game, something we'd practiced and trained for since August.

Mark Nentl had a very interesting observation on this game. Both teams had a fumble that led to a touchdown for the other team. Otherwise, the game was extremely close the entire time. Mark figured that in 1981 if Holdingford played Mahnomen 10 times, that the wins-loss record would likely be very close and every single game would be a one- or two-point difference. The teams were evenly matched and we were fortunate to win that one. Many players noted that the Mahnomen players were classy and good sportsmen after the game.

The coach of Mahnomen was Ken Baumann. He coached in Mahnomen from around 1969 until 2000. He had a career record, according to him, of 287-66-2. I have never met him, though I did speak to him over the phone. He reminds me a little of Coach Roebuck. He went into a small Minnesota town and turned the football program into a powerhouse. He won his first state title in 1980. He won four more titles in a row in the 1990s, and won his sixth state title in 1998. And his teams were runners up four times. Coach Baumann knew about winning.

After Holdingford beat his team in 1981, he came into our locker room to congratulate the team and coaches. He said to keep the title trophy in the North. He was all class. Incidentally, not everyone in the town of

Mahnomen was all class. Jim Ertl and others remember some little kids egging our bus as we left town. We did end their twenty-three-game win streak, after all.

STORY ALERT - LIFE IN THE 80s

The life of a high schooler in the early 1980s was pretty tame compared to nowadays. Bill Shank told a funny story illustrating some of the innocence of the time. Kids of the same age often hung out with each other, one of the things for high school kids from Holdingford to do was to go to St. Cloud. St. Cloud with about 40,000 residents was the biggest town in the area. St. Cloud also had the closest theatres and a drive-in theatre. It had things to do for bored country kids. Bill mentioned that they would take ivory bar soap and rub it on the windows of the girl's car. It clouded up the windows and you needed hot water to get it off. Which was tricky in the winter. One time they did the same to his front windshield and he had to drive home to Holdingford with his head out the window. To get the girls back for that time, Bill and the fellas put some Limburger cheese in the manifold of their car. Apparently when the engine heated up and the cheese heated up, it sent an especially pungent smell into the car.

Chapter 7 - The Championship Game

I'll point out again that the Mahnomen game was the semi-finals game. We still had another game against the winner of the Southern half of Minnesota. That team was Pine Island. If the Mahnomen game was the equivalent of conquering Mount Everest, then the championship game against Pine Island was like surviving the descent of Everest. The area around the summit of Everest is littered with bodies of people who have reached the summit but died going down. No one was going to die, but Coach Roebuck stressed that we couldn't let up the intensity.

Using Herb Brooks and 1980 Olympic hockey team analogy again, The Soviets had won Olympic gold the last four Olympics. They were heavily favored. Similar to us against Mahnomen. The American team finessed the Soviets and won with outstanding individual and team play and never-say-die attitude. They still had to play Finland for the Gold, and we still had to play Pine Island for our Trophy.

The Pine Island game was a bit of an unknown. Whereas with Mahnomen we knew what we were up against. Pine Island was a bit of a mystery. They won the southern half of Minnesota, which means they were the best of dozens of teams. I don't believe we had ever played them before, so we didn't know what to expect.

The coach prepared for the game with the same calm intensity he displayed all year. We went over statistics. We went over scenarios. He wanted the players in the right frame of mind.

Also, during this week before the Championship game, the weather turned really cold. We still had to practice after school. Everyone had ideas on how to stay warm in the freezing conditions. Some wore long johns under their pants. Someone suggested nylons. And some of us did both because it was so cold. I don't remember if nylons helped, but it is technically another layer of clothing. I'm not sure how I asked my mom for an old pair of nylons but since they never threw anything out there must have been an old pair lying around.

Around this time another funny thing happened in the locker room before practice. Some of us didn't get to dress for the playoff games but we still had to dress for practice.

Well, in the locker room most of us were layering up. Apparently sometime earlier in the season when it was 80-85 degrees out, Dan Stich boasted that he would never wear anything other than a t-shirt under his shoulder pads. On that extremely cold day before practice, I distinctly remember Stich putting on a long sleeve shirt, well Ron Feidler saw this as well and this certainly wouldn't do. He obviously remembered Stich saying he would never need to wear anything but a t-shirt. He said something to the effect of "You effing wimp I thought you said at the beginning of the year that you would never wear a long-sleeve shirt during the year. You said you would only ever wear a t-shirt…. are you going back on your word?"

This went back and forth for a while. Most of us would have simply said F-you it's cold outside, and just layered up. But not Dan Stich; after considering it, he must have remembered saying it, and true to his word, he took off the long-sleeve shirt and practiced in the t-shirt. And it was frigid cold out. I reminded Ron Fiedler of this story and true to form he explained, "that would be my job to call him out." Those two, never a dull moment.

If I recall correctly, he did get a break that week since some days were so cold, we had practice in the big bus garage or the gym.

The championship game was on a Friday night at 7:30 in Pine Island. The trip there was around 3 hours. We also stopped for a meal on the way there. So, we had to leave school around noon. This means we got out of class early which was a bonus. For normal away games during the year we road in yellow school buses. For the 2 away games during the playoffs we got to go in style. We rode in a motorcoach bus.

For away games Coach Roebuck also wanted us to look professional. He wanted everyone to dress up. No jeans. Dress pants and nice shirt and maybe jackets were required. We departed the school parking lot like warriors off to battle, to the cheers of the supporting students.

That week there was a big snow storm in Pine Island. Several inches of snow had fallen and the field had to be plowed and shoveled off. When we got there, the field was frozen with loose snow in places. This likely favored Pine Island so they probably didn't want to clean it too much. Their hope would have been that the icy field would slow down the mighty one-two punch of the Huskers' running attack.

Pine Island had a smart game plan. Their whole goal was to shut down our All-State running back, Brian Reis. And technically speaking, they almost did that. Perhaps more accurately, I could say that if their goal was to shut him down, what they sort of did was slow him down. He did get 182 yards rushing, but it took him twenty-three carries to do it. I believe that was his most carries in a game all year. During the year Brian Reis averaged over ten yards per carry. In this game his average was "only" 7.9 yards per carry and two touchdowns. If Pine Island was looking for a positive, maybe that is one.

The real shock to Pine Island may have been the game Dan Stich had. He was an all-conference full back with around 1,200 yards for the year. But his deeds may have been slightly overshadowed by the all-state numbers of Brian Reis. Dan Stich in his own right was an exceptional power runner, and he had break out speed to boot. He was a sprinter in track in the spring as well. If Pine Island's goal was to slow down Reis, then Stich may have been a surprise to them. Dan Stich carried the ball fourteen times for 246 yards and three touchdowns. Even on the slick and frozen field we ran all over them.

Holdingford had an incredibly effective option play. There was an option to Stich up the middle and if that wasn't open, then Dale Mehr would keep it and go to the outside with the option to give it to Brian Reis, or keep it himself. Since they keyed on Reis, it left Dan Stich open in the middle. And he was up the challenge. He averaged seventeen yards per carry.

Incidentally Mehr, Stich, and Reis were extremely polished and practiced with this play. You see, as Dale Mehr was optioning the ball to Stich up the middle he also was looking at and reading the linebackers and defenders. If he thought there was an opening, he would give the ball to Stich and fake that he kept it and go to the outside. If he didn't see on opportunity in the middle he would fake to Stich and pull the ball out and move to the outside. In that split second, he either handed off or he kept it. They intuitively had to do this without fumbling it. And they were velvety smooth. More than once during the season when Mehr faked it to Stich and then handed it off to Reis on the outside, Reis was running with the ball and the whistle blew because the Referee thought he handed it off to Stich and Stich was tackled in the middle. They faked out the defense and the refs. The whistle blew so Reis had to stop running and the play was over.

Keep in mind as a sophomore during practice we were sometimes thrown in to play defense against the first team offense. Practices were usually run at three-quarter speed. Which means not 100% full contact. Thank God! This was to prevent injuries in practice. We often had to try to tackle these guys as they came through the line. Whereas Brian Reis was lightning quick with his cuts and then sprinter fast as he flew past you, I remember feeling lucky if I got a hand on his Jersey as he accelerated by. Dan Stich on the other hand was more of a power runner with unusual speed for a full back. Trying to tackle him during practice was a little like jumping in front of a runaway horse. The horse barely slows down as you hear a thump, you feel some pain, on your back you look up at the bright blue sky, and try to convince yourself that he is lucky you are only going at three-quarter speed…

Sophomore Tim Kolstad mentioned that sometimes in practice he had to block against Senior Dan Bieniek. He claims that Dan never got the memo that we practiced at ¾ speed. He claims Dan was always going at 100%.

As Correspondent Dennis Shapiro wrote in the Minneapolis Tribune, "There was nothing surprising in Holdingford's Style. Nothing tricky. And there was nothing Pine Island could do to stop it."

Dan Stich opened the scoring in the first quarter with a 35-yard touchdown run. Soon after he added another with a 26-yard run. Still later in the first quarter Brian Reis scored on a 13-yard run. No one scored in the second quarter and the game went into the half 20-0. During halftime there was excitement in the air. We were dominating and things looked good. Coach Roebuck said in the halftime speech that we needed to get at least one more touchdown. In the third quarter Dan Stich scored his third touchdown on a 60-yard run. We weren't quite done yet. In the fourth quarter Dale Mehr scored on a 1-yard quarterback sneak. Reis scored again late in the fourth quarter.

The mighty Huskers won this game 39-0. As Pine Island fell behind early, they started to pass more often. The stiff Huskers defense was up to the challenge. The defense intercepted Pine Island 4 times and Lee Odden recovered a fumble. As we were ahead early, a lot of the bench players got in to play in this game. As the game was well in hand the shoulder slaps and congratulations started in the 4th quarter. Then the game was over. The mighty Huskers were State Champions.

And the celebration began.

The population of Holdingford at this time was around a little over six-hundred. By most accounts, there were at least this many people on our side of the field. There were eleven greyhound buses for adults. I believe there were a bunch of yellow school buses full of students. And there were many cars as well.

As a player on the team, I was on the sideline. Per state rules only a certain number of players were allowed to dress, (around 40). The other fifteen or so of us were on the sideline as part of the team, though wearing our civilian clothes.

As the final second ticked off everyone rushed the field. It was pandemonium. This was the biggest sports victory for Holdingford ever. Everyone was running around hugging everyone. It was wild. It was a celebration. Dan Stich and Lee Oden and others left the field after the game to go to the locker room. Because that is what we did all year. After a while when no one else showed up, they came back to the field to see the party was still going. Everyone wanted to soak in the moment and just maintain the excitement of our state title victory. The celebration continued for some time. There was joy and laughter. There were congratulations and hugs from the appreciative fans. There were interviews for the coaches and star players. For Coach Roebuck it was the pinnacle of his decade and half of coaching. Maybe even a bit of vindication that his style of coaching was rewarded with the highest achievement a high school coach strives for. The Huskers were finally State Champions.

Slowly, people headed back to their bus or car for the ride home. The players headed to the locker room to shower and change, and board the bus for our ride home. I don't think any little kids egged our bus in Pine Island.

I don't remember if we stopped for food on the way home or not. I don't recall any exciting details of the bus ride home. The seats weren't comfortable and it was late and it was probably a three-hour ride. Irv Pierskalla recalls sleeping up top where the luggage would normally go.

But I do remember something that happened before we got home. This was around one o'clock in the morning. As we were approaching Holdingford from the South, about 5 miles outside of town the bus went through a smaller town called St. Anna. It is a town with a church, a bar, and a gas station. As the bus slowed down to pass through the town, on either side of the road there were cars parked facing the road. As they saw the bus coming, they hit their lights and honked their horns. It was the Holdingford fans. It was a thoughtful gesture for them to stay up late to welcome us home. As I mentioned, the people in town didn't want the celebration to end so they set up this impromptu welcome home light and honk show. As the bus went through, all the cars filed in behind and we led the parade the last five miles into the high school parking lot, where, you may have guessed, the celebration continued. Winning the state title in Football was the biggest thing to happen in Holdingford in a long, long time. People wanted to savor the moment.

Coach Roebuck could have run for mayor. He brought this title to our town. There were some talented players on the team, but Coach Roebuck molded the team into champions. It wasn't just a victory for the school, it was a victory for the town. And the town wanted to continue the party. Coach Roebuck said some words there in the parking lot. There may have been other speakers. But it was about 2:30.

The love and support the town showed toward the football team that night and all season was incredible.

Even the next day there was another impromptu celebration in the gym. Everyone wanted to savor the moment and extend the jubilation. The excitement was palpable. The joy was contagious and the energy was infectious. What a season to remember. A perfect season!

In the morning, after a few hours of sleep, we were dressed up in our Sunday best (it was a Saturday) to meet at the gym for the awards ceremony. There were several hundred people in the bleachers. As the *St. Cloud Times* paper stated: the team managers walked in carrying the big trophy. Student managers were Kevin Caspers, Steve Stoermann, Eric Fiedler, Chuck Doucet, and Ron Huls. They were followed by all the players, coaches, and cheerleaders. The crowd stood and cheered, the first of eight standing ovations. The town, the people, the players, all wanted to relish this moment. There were speeches, there were jokes, and there were stories. The exact details may be a bit vague, but I do remember something funny Coach Roebuck said. Something to the effect that he has been smiling a lot since winning the game the night before. Smiling in the locker room, smiling on the bus, smiling at breakfast, and according to his wife Jane, he was even smiling in his sleep.

When you factor in all the high school teams in the state of Minnesota, it is rare for a Coach to win a State Championship. I don't believe it happens by accident. If it happens it is usually after years of coaching, after some trial and errors, and after serious study and a lot of extra hours. By this time Coach Roebuck had been coaching for over 15 years. This is a major accomplishment for any football coach. He won a state championship and that was a huge achievement. He deserves much credit.

STORY ALERT - LIFE IN THE 80s

As mentioned, our little home town has about 621 residents. In the winter, there wasn't much to do. On weekends friends and I would go to St. Cloud for a movie or go bowling or something. One time we went to a movie and snuck in a couple bottles of beer. Someone in the group (Dan Fiedler I believe) finished the bottle (with a straw) and set it on the floor in the theatre. Sometime later during a quiet part of the movie the bottle got knocked over and made a loud clanking noise on the hard floor and then rolled downhill in the theatre. Everyone in the theatre started hooting and laughing.

BONUS STORY

Tim Kolstad and another classmate Bobby Young had a couple hobbies back in high school. They liked to work on cars and occasionally make moonshine. Making moonshine was not illegal, and really not that hard to do. There are recipes everywhere. Back then I tasted it, and it was some strong stuff. One shot was all one needed. As I was reminiscing with Tim, I asked if he ever used it as gas. In fact, he did in their lawnmower. It worked fairly well for a while, until the lawn mower blew up.

DOUBLE BONUS STORY

Speaking of Tom Kolstad. This event actually happened after we graduated, sometime in the mid 1980s. My friend Shawn Kollodge and I were visiting my cousin Pat Klepaida out in the country. He had a big old red car that worked but was on its last leg. He joked that he wanted to make a convertible out of it. I asked, are you sure? Sure, he said. I said let me do some checking around. Shawn and I jumped into the red car and went about 2 miles to Tim Kolstad's house. Tim scratched his chin and gave it a look. He was up to the challenge. He conveniently had a torch right there in the garage and went to work. Less than an hour later we had a convertible. Back at my cousins we pulled up with the roof in the back seat. Within an hour we made the car a convertible. I don't think my cousin actually expected us to come back with the roof off. It still had some rough edges. But we ended up driving that car for a couple summers.

Chapter 8 – After

And so, after the "Perfect Season" the school year went on. There was a party for all the players and students one weekend soon after the season ended. This I believe was at Dan Dickhausen's house. There was beer. There was music. There were probably some broken things. Just a normal high school party to celebrate.

A lot of these same athletes joined the basketball team or wrestling team as their winter sport. Then in the Spring they played baseball or participated in track. Many were three sport athletes. The seniors graduated in early June of 1982. Their class song was, "Time for me to fly," by REO Speedwagon. But I think it should have been: "We are the Champions" by Queen. Because this class will be champions forever.

In the spring of 1982, it was announced that Coach Roebuck was the Class B Coach of the Year. Then at the Banquet of the coach's association it was announced that he was voted the Coach of the Year for all coaches in all of Minnesota. So that included all the coaches of all the classes, even the bigger schools. What a tremendous honor for Coach Roebuck. His peers recognized him for his "Perfect Season."

The seniors went on to either jobs or college. Some went into the military. Dan Gill spent 20 years in the Air Force. Then another 20 years as a cop in Alaska.

Dale Mehr, the quarterback, went on to start for four years at the University of Minnesota Morris and set all kinds of passing records there. And it should be noted he signed with the Minnesota Vikings and was eventually cut before the regular season started as the fourth quarterback. Certainly, a major accomplishment.

Dan stich went to play for St. Cloud State, though as the story goes, during the first few weeks of practice, he set upon and laid a "hellacious" tackle on the runner, and injured his neck and never played football again. Physically he was undersized perhaps to play division II, but by measuring with the heart he was a giant. He had the heart and instinct of an NFL player, but at around 170 lbs he may have been a little undersized. As a high school player, he was a legend, though.

Brian Reis got a scholarship to play for St. Cloud State, and could have joined his teammate Dan Stich there but before the year started, he decided to give up football. Years later, I asked him about this, and he said that he had some shoulder injuries and didn't want to aggravate these injuries. In high school he was an all-state player and exceptional at that level. However, perhaps going to the next level he would only have been a mid-level player, and the health risk for him wasn't worth it.

Jim Ertl with his brother Bill took over the family farm.

Ron Fiedler eventually moved to Florida where he currently resides.

Others got jobs or continued with their education.

Several former players are successful business owners.

Tim Kolstad does not have a cell phone, and is not on Facebook.

Many of the players still live around Minnesota, and quite a few reside in the Holdingford area.

Some players still golf together.

Assistant Coach Roman Pierskalla has an interesting perspective. He graduated from Holdingford a few years earlier. He played football for Coach Roebuck and Coach Bruns. He had a lot of respect for them and claims they were the reason he got into education. After getting his college degree he was hired back at Holdingford to teach. He then became an assistant to the Coach he played for a few years previous.

STORY ALERT - LIFE IN THE 80s

This occurred later in the same school year in the spring of 1982. The seniors usually take some sort of class trip before they graduate in early June. It happens each spring. Some trips are one day and some can be an overnight trip. The seniors that year took an overnight trip. I have been told that sometimes the seniors try to sneak alcohol on these trips. Some are more successful than others. This is just an example of the thing's kids did back in the early 80s.

It was a two-day trip, and they left on a Tuesday (I can't remember which day it was but both days were during the school week.) These trips were usually held at a resort of some type that could handle 100 or so kids and chaperones. They left early in the morning. Well, all of a sudden, two seniors show up back at school. Ken Opatz and Dan Bieniek. They got sent home from the class trip. As the story goes, there must have been a liquor store near the resort. These 2 seniors went there and with a very good fake ID were able to buy some alcohol. However, the store clerk was suspicious and he notified the resort or the chaperones. He explained that they had a good ID but he was skeptical all the same. (After he got the money.) He described the two as: One was wearing a jacket with the name Ken on it and the other had a speech impediment. (Dan Bieniek wore a hearing aid and has a bit of a speech impediment, though he is easily understandable.) Anyone who was familiar with the senior class immediately knew who the culprits were. Their two-day class trip turned into a two-hour visit to the resort, and back to school they went. And I assume their alcohol was confiscated. Young boys will be boys.

CHAPTER 9 - Coach Roebuck's Legacy

I will admit that in the course of interviewing people, not everyone was as fond of the Coach as most of us. Maybe some people didn't like all the conditioning. Maybe some didn't get to play as much as they would have liked. Heck, I didn't get to play as much as I would have liked. Maybe they got yelled at and didn't appreciate that. Well, not everyone is a fan of George Washington or Abe Lincoln. But most would agree that those two presidents were able, honest, and great at their job. And like Coach Roebuck, they will not soon be forgotten for what they achieved in their respective fields. (Beneficial pun simply a bonus.)

As I've been saying, Coach Roebuck was often a positive and soothing influence on us players. In fact, my next story captures another likely first for some of these guys. This happened the following season after we won the state title, when our team was struggling and our record was under 500. After another disappointing loss in a season full of disappointing losses, in the locker room the coach said to us players, " I love you guys." For a lot of the players this may have been the first time someone said that to them. In our stoic and repressed little town in the 80s parents were not as expressive. (I did hear it once in the second grade. Unfortunately, I didn't reciprocate the sentiments. I wanted to meet other people.) That year I think we had heart and we tried. A lot of our losses were by only a couple points. But that team could not match the success of the previous year. The 1982 team ended with a record of 4-5.

Incidentally, when I was a senior, we had a very good team. We were 8-1. We didn't go to the playoffs because the team we lost too, Kimball, was 9-0. They got the one playoff spot. Perhaps that's another story...

Coach Roebuck was the football coach in Holdingford for fifteen years. He coached hundreds of Holdingford players. Several of my older brothers played for him. Everyone knew him. Not all perhaps liked him but most respected him. Coaches aren't always liked by their players. Football is a team sport and the coach needs to maintain order and discipline. The coach is a teacher with a goal to help the individual player play better, which makes the team better, which leads to victory.

As I spoke to some players Coach Roebuck had his way of doing things. He was the coach. He had the responsibility, so he made the rules. That is just how it is. Most of us farm kids unconsciously understood this. When I say unconsciously, I just mean we never thought to question what we were being told. Coach said to do something this way, most never took a minute to ponder the directive, we simply did what we were told to do. Mark Petron equated it to the same respect and fear we have of our parents.

And so as in anything there will always be people who probably didn't appreciate being told what to do, or didn't appreciate being told to run extra laps, or didn't appreciate being yelled at, or thought they should be playing more. As a bit of a student of football, I understand that even if you have superior talent or athletic ability, but you are not a team player, or you don't do your job on each play, you may not fit in some football programs. Hopefully Coach Roebuck understood kids are kids and did not worry about some who didn't enjoy their time as players on the team.

Another thing: a lot of the kids who played during these years were farm kids. And most likely their parents were farm kids. The parents were authority figures but outside of home there wasn't much guidance. Coach Roebuck filled a void. Kids without much to do tend to find things to do, and it is not always productive or positive things. In central Minnesota there were lots of parties, lots of drinking. Players on the team have rules while on the team (inside and outside of school). One of those rules was no drinking. Get caught drinking and you may get suspended from the team. That was enough for me. I thoroughly enjoyed my years playing football, and I didn't want to jeopardize playing so I stayed away from parties and alcohol (during the season). So having rules and consequences is just another life lesson. I don't recall that rule as being a problem.

I'll remember Coach Roebuck as a calm ship captain during a raging storm. He rarely, if ever, had to raise his voice. He had a rare talent or ability when talking to us players; we didn't contemplate whether he was an expert at pass-blocking or route-running. We didn't think about what was happening in class tomorrow, or if the cows were getting milked... or at least I didn't ... we listened and did exactly what we were told to do.

He had the rare combination of confidence and leadership so that when he said something, no one doubted it, no one questioned it, he conveyed a singular confidence. We were young and dumb and naive. We were there to play football and learn. We assumed rightfully he knew what he was talking about. Based on hindsight we have all had coaches who didn't know what the hell they were talking about. They were there to collect an extra paycheck to supplement their teaching salary. They didn't put in extra time to learn the sport, or to be better at relating with students. Coach Roebuck had the same talent as coaches like Bill Belichick or Phil Jackson. It is an innate skill: that when they spoke you listened because of their reputation for winning.

Like if Albert Einstein were explaining physics to you. You may not completely understand what he was talking about, but you knew with absolute certainty that he knew what he was talking about.

There is elegance in playing a sport you enjoy for an excellent coach: You volunteer to be exercised, disciplined, strengthened, and hopefully improved. The upside is that you receive all those things. And the down side is the exact same thing, you receive all those things.

Coach Roebuck may not have remembered every player who played for him, but every player will remember him. For most, he was a strong, positive force, someone who emphasized work ethic, professionalism, and teamwork in football. For some he was a coach and a man that you didn't want to disappoint because he took the time to make you a better player and ultimately a better person. And for a few he left a lifelong impression. Someone who you may compare leaders and other coaches to. He had a style. It's high school football, and since he never wanted to coach at a higher level, his goals were genuine. He wasn't in it for fame and fortune. But simply to make a team of eleven individuals on the field the best they could be. To teach how when individuals work together, they can win as a team. Similar to the great college basketball coach John Wooden, whose goal was for his players to individually reach their highest potential, and as a team work as a perfect unit. When they do that, they will win. Though winning wasn't the goal.

Perfection was the goal. Perfection in team sports isn't usually attainable, but when you constantly strive for perfection, the result is often victory. That is something Vince Lombardi aspired to, as he is quoted:

"Perfection is not attainable, but if we chase perfection, we can catch excellence."

Speaking of John Wooden, he said something on a podcast once that I heard that I think, sums up Coach Roebuck as it relates to leading by example. Wooden said this was a quote from the 1930s. He doesn't give an author:

"No written word, no spoken plea,
Can teach our youth what they should be,
nor all the books on all the shelves,
It's what the Teachers are themselves."

Coach Roebuck was the kind of coach you didn't want to let down or disappoint. When he said to do something, you did it; you wanted to prove that his faith in you was justified.

He demonstrated to us how to be a proper leader. He taught us that winning is not an accident but can be a habit, based on preparation, practice, and teamwork. He illustrated that you can win with honor and integrity. There are no shortcuts or cutting corners, but a formula for success. He also explained that even when doing these things there is no guarantee of success. But you do things right anyway because winning by cheating is a hollow win.

Winning is not everything, honor and integrity is everything. And most of all, he taught us that when you do all these things, prepare, practice, condition, go 100%, never quit, that sometimes you create your own luck, and when the season is over, you are undefeated champions.

Those habits also translate to life after sports. Scott Lange mentioned that when talking with the coach about sports and life he had a way of making you do the right thing without saying it. Dan Fiedler said the same thing. He said the coach had a way of teaching you about life. Gary Wentland said he always gave good advice. Eugene Ostendorf said the Coach tried to bring out the best of every player. Jim Ertl mentioned that he held you to higher standards. Frank Stewart said he built a sense of camaraderie. Dan Gill said he was fair and professional. Ron Pierskalla recalls the coach was good about congratulating you on a good play and coaching you up on mistakes, and also pushing you to perform one level up from where you were. Sam Pierskalla said he treated everyone fair and equally. Greg Konsor mentioned that he wanted everyone to achieve their best. These sentiments were echoed by others as well.

Coach Roebuck was the type of person that when explaining a football concept or philosophy most wouldn't question his opinion. When it came to football, his knowledge was inherent to his character. His knowledge of football was innate. As compared to some other coaches whose knowledge was inane or lacking any sense. This is visible in all levels of sports but can be especially apparent in high school, since coaching for some in high school is simply a way to earn some extra money. In seventh and eighth grade sports, the coach is usually just an adult supervisor. The game is still about having fun and learning and letting everyone participate.

In those younger grades the students and the coach knew they weren't sport-specific experts. A smart coach wouldn't try to be something more than they were. It would be about having fun. They would admit it if they didn't know a certain rule or something. However, once you get to varsity level even the students expect a little bit more knowledge from the coach. It should still be about having fun, but we should also be learning something new each day.

Think about what a high school football coach is up against. Their job is to take a teachable but undisciplined, strong but unfocused, talented but independent group of eleven players and on each play teach them to do their separate but crucial job, in order to have a successful play. And to maintain that discipline and structure for four quarters. That takes a passion.

The beauty of Coach Roebuck was that he had put in so much extra study of the game that he was an expert. Dale Mehr and Greg Konsor both mentioned that the coach devoted hours of time behind the scenes to designing plays and studying the art of football. His expertise was obvious. And he understood that winning can become a habit. In that year 1981, a lot of us on the team had older siblings who had played for Coach Roebuck. The respect he had earned was passed down. So, when we finally were able to play with the varsity team, every player knew without a doubt that Coach

Roebuck was the authority on this game. His knowledge of the game was vast, and his understanding of what it took to win was instinctive. His methods were not questioned. And Coach Roebuck was of such high character and honor that he never abused that trust. He taught that when you practice correctly and improve a little daily, winning is the result. In contrast to Coaches of low moral character who abuse the power they are given and fake their way through coaching. They tend to need to yell or inflict punishment to prove their authority.

By most accounts Coach Roebuck rarely raised his voice and seldom if ever cursed. He had the elusive quality of commanding respect on the football field. Similar to the respect General Dwight Eisenhower or General Norman Schwartzkopf likely had on a battlefield.

Coaching may be a little like being a general on the battlefield. One needs to be calm and cool, absorbing all the info coming in, synthesizing that info and making the best decision based on known factors. Football is a complicated chess game. Eleven players on each side of the ball. Some are doing their job correctly, some not. The other coach is trying to surprise and outsmart you. And the Coach as a leader, gives direction, sets plays, but the players have to execute the play, all the while the eleven players on the other side of the ball are trying to disrupt your plan.

There is beauty in football. When a play is executed perfectly and all eleven players do their job properly, and your running back breaks open to score a touchdown, there is beauty in that.

Though keep in mind that winning is not always the result. No team simply goes undefeated forever. Consider that he had another quality of relating football to life. Since this is small town America, not too many players go on to play professional sports. These two or three years of varsity football is just a small blip in our overall lives. His lesson was that though winning is not always the result and perfection may not be attainable, doing your best and giving your all are qualities that will benefit you for the remainder of your life. That may be the most important legacy he imparted on his players.

THE END

The Holdingford Huskers football team won another State Championship in 2014.

In the class of 1982 Yearbook (Annual), there was a blurb written by the staff, attributed to the yearbook staff:

"The 1981 Husker football team accomplished the dream of every team, a state championship and an undefeated season. While the team possessed the obvious skills of excellent blocking, ball-handling, and team speed, it also possessed the not so obvious ingredients of togetherness and a strong desire to succeed. Each player seemed to take special pride for what he could do best, which made everyone feel a sense of importance to the team's success. Never did any player allow his personal goals and needs to interfere with the team goals and needs. Since the 1981 squad seemed to dedicate themselves to a total team effort, that attitude may have been the major contribution to the great season that we all enjoyed. Also, never before has the school spirit been as high, nor the student body been as supportive of the football team; a tribute to the great accomplishment of becoming State Champions. "

Acknowledgements

    I would like to thank all the players who contributed their stories and memories to this book. Especially Jim Ertl who, whenever someone said they weren't sure about something, to ask Jim Ertl. I would like to thank Dan Stich's mom, Annette Stich, who kept a scrapbook with newspaper clipping and articles and made it available to me, which I used extensively for this book.

Team photo. 1981. From Yearbook.

Dale Mehr running against Mahnomen. Brian Danzl leading the way. Brian Reis looking for a possible pitch. From Yearbook.

Defense swarms Mahnomen runner. Lee Odden (57) and Brian Danzl (79) and others look to make tackle. From Yearbook.

Dan Stich hitting the open field. From Yearbook.

Brian Danzl after fumble recovery against Mahnomen. From Yearbook.

Dan Sobieck (82), Mark Nentl (75), Ron Pierskalla (86) celebrate Brian Danzl's fumble recovery run. From Yearbook.

The scoreboard at Mahnomen. 21-14. From Yearbook.

Coach Roebuck on the sideline of a game. From Yearbook.

Coach Roebuck during a game. From Yearbook.

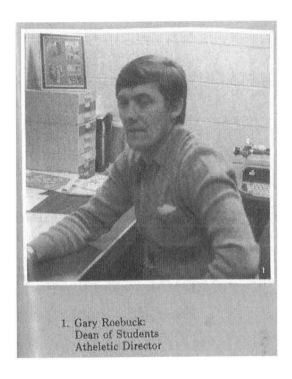

1. Gary Roebuck:
Dean of Students
Atheletic Director

Coach Roebuck at his day job as school Dean and Athletic Director. From Yearbook.

Some fans made this. It traveled to the playoff away games. From Yearbook.

Dale Mehr looking to pass against Pine Island. From Yearbook.

Dan Stich into open field against Pine Island. From Yearbook.

Lee Odden recovers fumble at Pine Island. From Yearbook.

Players celebrate the Championship at Pine Island. From Yearbook.

Fans swarm the field to celebrate the win. From Yearbook.

Players can finally raise the Championship trophy. From Yearbook.

That's all, folks! #32

Made in the USA
Middletown, DE
15 September 2021